Employment effects
of multinational enterprises
in industrialised countries

Employment effects of multinational enterprises in industrialised countries

International Labour Office   Geneva

ISBN 92-2-102741-4

First published 1981

Printed in Switzerland

PREFACE

The present report is a synthesis of findings relating to industrialised countries of a research project on the employment effects of multinational enterprises in home and host countries undertaken by the ILO's Multinational enterprises programme (MULTI). This report will be complemented by a similar synthesis report on developing countries.[1] A number of component studies on particular countries, regions and selected themes have already been issued as working papers.[2]

The aim of the research project was to study in detail an area which an earlier preliminary study[3] has shown to be of particular interest to ILO constituents. It is evident, however, that despite the considerable efforts which have been made in gathering relevant material and the important co-operation received from many quarters, a report on such a complex and dynamic area cannot be definitive.

The present report is intended as a stock-taking exercise of the major aspects to be considered when evaluating the employment impact of multinational enterprises (MNEs) in the industrialised world. It should provide a sound basis, it is hoped, for discussions in and outside the ILO. At the same time, because of data limitations or methodological reasons and the need to focus on questions of particular interest to the ILO constituency it has not been possible to give equal treatment to all areas potentially falling under the broad theme of the investigation.

The report mainly provides information on the direct employment effects of MNEs. It highlights the employment trends in MNEs, compared with over-all employment development and with such trends in manufacturing or for the specific industries where data were available. It also analyses the employment of MNEs in their home countries, the employment importance of foreign enterprises, and the development of MNE home-country employment in comparison with the expansion of MNE employment in foreign countries, including developing countries. Furthermore, it reviews the sectoral distribution and employment evolution of MNEs. Finally, information is provided on skill-mix and structure, employment stability and employment repercussions in MNEs and the international restructuring of industry together with indications of the role played by MNEs in this process. This includes a relatively extensive treatment of the "employment export" and "job export" issues, which are of particular interest in the context of industrialised countries.

---

[1] ILO: Employment effects of multinational enterprises in developing countries (Geneva, forthcoming 1981).

[2] See list of these working papers in Appendix I.

[3] ILO: The impact of multinational enterprises on employment and training (Geneva, 1976).

On the other hand, less attention has been given in the present report, to the indirect employment effects of MNEs mainly for reasons of data availability and methodological difficulty. Moreover, the issue appears to be of special interest primarily in the context of developing countries. Consequently, these indirect employment effects are treated in more detail in the companion report on developing countries, especially those occurring through backward and forward input/output linkages with host country economies. The policy problems raised in this connection have likewise been highlighted there. Other indirect employment effects (such as those resulting from income creation, the impact of MNEs on public budgets, balance of payments, etc.), have not been dealt with in either report as no reliable quantitative information on these could be obtained on a world-wide basis. However, some of the component studies refer to such employment effects for individual countries.

A considerable amount and variety of inputs have been used for the present report, including special surveys, component reports and other studies (specifically commissioned or already available from earlier research), as shown in the graph on p.vii. Valuable co-operation has been received from governments, national and inter-national trade union and employer circles, including a number of multinational enterprises, and from various researchers and research institutions, for which the ILO expresses its appreciation. The research project received financial support from the Government of the Netherlands, the Central Union of Swiss Employers' Associations and the International Confederation of Free Trade Unions, which is gratefully acknowledged.

The study was co-ordinated by Lawrence G. Franko, Geneva, formerly associated with the Harvard Multinational Enterprise Project. Research assistance throughout the project was furnished by Paul Bailey, University of Munich (he is also the author of one of the component studies), and for the initial phases of the project by Marie-Claire Bussat, University of Savoie (Chambéry). The project benefited from the counsel of a Technical Advisory Group constituted of senior officials of the Employment and Development Department of the ILO and other departments. In addition, a number of technical consultations were held with outside specialists.

INPUTS FOR STUDY ON
EMPLOYMENT EFFECTS OF MULTINATIONAL ENTERPRISES
IN INDUSTRIALISED COUNTRIES

```
┌─────────────────────────┐
│     SYNTHESIS REPORT     │
└─────────────────────────┘
```

Survey among Labour Ministries in 26 industrialised home and host countries of multinational enterprises (Europe, North America,
Japan, Australia and New Zealand)

Information requested through international
employers' and workers' organisations and
their affiliates

Component studies prepared for project, in
particular those for: Belgium, Sweden, United
States of America, United Kingdom and the
Federal Republic of Germany; and other
special ILO studies, such as working papers
of the ILO's Employment and Development
Department

Analysis of relevant literature and
documents, including information requested
from specialised research institutions, and
statistical data contained in UN, EEC and
OECD publications

TABLE OF CONTENTS

CHAPTER I

TRENDS IN DIRECT EMPLOYMENT IN
MULTINATIONAL ENTERPRISES IN INDUSTRIALISED COUNTRIES

Introduction

By any standards, and however defined, multinational enterprises (MNEs) are major employers in the industrialised world. Majority-owned subsidiaries of foreign companies alone accounted for a fifth or more of the manufacturing employees in at least seven industrialised market economy countries (IMEC) in 1975 and more than a tenth in nine, according to OECD figures and other sources. If, as a global estimate requires, employment in home-country operations of multinational manufacturing firms is taken into account as well, multinationals account for over 40 per cent of industrial employment in nine of the wealthiest industrialised nations (see tables I.3 and I.4). This is the case even under conservative definitions of the number of foreign production subsidiaries which firms must have in order to be considered multinational.

A project carried out jointly by Harvard University and the Center for Education in International Management (CEI), Geneva, estimated that, in 1972, the 400 largest MNEs in the manufacturing industry alone (defined as enterprises with manufacturing facilities in seven or more countries) employed some 30 million people throughout the world.[1]

In a special survey for the year 1973, the Commission of the European Communities[2] found almost 46 million employees in multinational enterprises world-wide (both in home and host countries).[3] The survey related to some 10,000 MNEs (about half of which, including the largest, were able to furnish employment data) and covered not only the manufacturing industry, but also the service sector, especially banking and insurance. The definition of a multinational enterprise adopted by the EEC covered all enterprises with at least one subsidiary in a foreign country. An analysis of the 260 largest MNEs from this sample, showed that they alone employed some 25 million persons in 1973 (for further details see tables I.1 and I.2).

If one assumes MNE employment in developing countries to be in the order of some 4 million workers[4], it can be posited that the order of magnitude of MNE employment in industrialised countries in mid-1970 was in the nature of 25-30 million (depending on the definition of multinational enterprises adopted). This estimate would correspond to approximately one-third of the employment in the manufacturing industry in the industrialised market economy countries (according to OECD data which place total manufacturing employment at some 90 million). The employment provided by MNEs would probably rise by another 10 million, if a rough estimate for employees in multinational service enterprises, such as in banking, insurance, hotel and retailing chains and advertising agencies, etc. were added.[5] These global estimates for industrialised countries accord well with available country-by-country foreign penetration data of the OECD[6] and the home-country MNE employment data contained in government memoranda received for the present study[7] (presented in tables I.3 and I.4).

Table I.1:   Estimates of world-wide direct employment in
             multinational enterprises (in the early 1970s)

	Number employed
EEC ESTIMATES	
For 5,105 multinationals[1] (in manufacturing and services e.g., banking, insurance, etc.)	45 983 914
In the 260 largest thereof	25 113 211
HARVARD-CEI PROJECT ESTIMATES	
For the 400 largest OECD-based manufacturing multinationals[2]	30 000 000

Sources: Commission of the European Communities: Survey of
           multinational enterprises, Vol.I (Brussels 1976), p.3.
           Harvard-CEI multinational enterprises project
           estimate, as reported in Lawrence G. Franko: Multi:
           national enterprise, the international division of
           labour in manufactures, and the developing countries
           (Geneva, ILO, 1975; mimeographed World Employment
           Programme research working paper; restricted
           distribution).

   [1] Estimates are for 1973 and refer to all enterprises
       with one or more foreign production facilities
       being multinational.

   [2] Estimates are for 1972 and define MNEs as enter-
       prises with manufacturing facilities in seven or
       more countries.

Over-all trends in employment

During the post-war decades preceding the recession of the mid-
1970s and especially during the 1960s, which probably witnessed the
most rapid MNE expansion, the majority of the main industrialised
countries experienced not only a considerable increase in their
per capita incomes, but also of the total number of jobs in their
economies (see table I in the Annex to this chapter).

Even during that era of economic and employment growth, however,
employment in manufacturing was increasing in absolute terms only in
a few industrialised countries, such as the United States, Canada,
France and Italy. In a number of other such countries, e.g. Sweden,
the Federal Republic of Germany, the Netherlands and the United
Kingdom, over-all employment in manufacturing was declining even
during this general growth period (see table II in the Annex to this
chapter). After the period of 1973/74, manufacturing employment
declined generally in most of the developed market economy countries
through 1979 (see Annex table II) except for Canada and the United
States of America.

Table I.2: Employees in multinationals world-wide
by country of origin of enterprise (1973)

Country of origin	Number of enterprises for which information is available	Per cent of total number of enterprises surveyed	Total employees world-wide	Per cent of total world-wide MNE employment
BELGIUM	170	67.5	491 218	1.1
DENMARK	82	59.9	165 216	0.4
FRANCE	424	75.0	3 357 133	7.3
GERMANY (FED.REP.)	994	81.3	5 409 369	11.7
IRELAND	29	90.6	91.217	0.2
ITALY	87	40.8	1 626 668	3.5
LUXEMBOURG	7	12.5	35 053	0.1
NETHERLANDS	240	53.1	1 831 849	4.0
UNITED KINGDOM	1 088	68.5	7 937 152	17.3
TOTAL EEC	3 129	69.0	20 962 875	45.6
AUSTRALIA	73	32.0	415 058	0.9
AUSTRIA	26	50.0	152 051	0.3
CANADA	97	36.2	755 328	1.6
FINLAND	39	76.5	164 316	0.4
HONG KONG	5	20.8	23 456	0.1
JAPAN	159	75.4	1 717 851	3.7
LICHTENSTEIN	1	1.1	3 724	-
MALAYSIA	2	1.1	576	-
NEW ZEALAND	24	20.5	61 177	0.1
NORWAY	83	63.8	118 362	0.3
PHILIPPINES	2	50.0	28.419	0.1
PORTUGAL	3	3.0	6 550	-
SINGAPORE	7	10.1	3 851	-
SPAIN	8	22.9	39 806	0.1
SWEDEN	231	76.7	1 054 303	2.3
UNITED STATES	1 073	41.8	19 592 054	42.6
TOTAL OTHER COUNTRIES	1 976	39.9	25 021 039	54.4
GRAND TOTAL	5 105	53.8	45 983 914	100.0

Source: EEC: Survey of multinational enterprises, op. cit., p. 33.
It should be noted, however, that the figures have not been
calculated on uniform bases. It must also be noted that
the fact that the enterprises for which employment data are
available represent only 53 per cent of the MNEs identified
in the EEC survey tends to understate the total direct
employment effect. On the other hand, only employees in
subsidiaries, in which the parent enterprise holds more than
50 per cent of the shares, have been counted. As the replies
received were incomplete the survey has not identified a valid
statistical sample from which general conclusions can be
accurately drawn concerning the wider picture.

On the other hand, after 1973, even with a low-growth economic situation, employment in the economy as a whole still either increased somewhat, as in the United States, Canada, Italy, Japan and Sweden, or tended to stagnate as in most other industrialised market economy countries. Only in the Federal Republic of Germany and Switzerland did substantial decreases occur in total employment during that period (along with some labour force contraction) (see Annex table II). Where net new employment occurred after 1973, or where total employment dropped at a slower rate than in manufacturing, the new employment often tended to be in services[8], primarily in private sector services, as shown particularly by the cases of Japan, the United States and Canada, but also in government services, as best illustrated in the United Kingdom.

Some of this new employment, including jobs replacing those disappearing from manufacturing, has been accounted for by service-sector multinationals. However, much of it, at least in the United States[9] and Canadian[10] cases, appears to have occurred in small, fairly new, locally-operating enterprises.

As relatively little research has been done on employment in multinational service industries it is impossible to substantiate further the role of these enterprises in the above-mentioned employment trends. This relative neglect in studies and statistics may be partly explained by the fact that the concern of labour and also of some governments is mainly related to problems associated with manufacturing jobs. Hence:

> .... the 'job' or 'labour' issue surrounding the MNC [Multinational Corporation] is largely a manufacturing industry phenomenon, in both the investing and recepient countries. Aside from problems such as labour standards and working conditions, which are found in all industries and in all countries, the principal concern of labour is the actual or potential ability of the MNC to change the 'locations' of its labour-using operations. This ability is practically non-existent in the extractive and primary commodity industries and in most services, such as whole-sale and retail trade, finance, tourism, transportation, communications and power. In these non-manufacturing activities there is (or should be) no real concern over the destruction of local jobs by MNC investments or over any expected advantage of the MNC in collective bargaining deriving from its status as a multinational. There may be a few exceptions to this general statement in vertically integrated industries, such as petroleum and rubber products, where the location of refining and processing must be solved. But even here the processing frequently is very capital (as opposed to labour) intensive and relatively small in comparison to the labour used in extraction, marketing and engineering. Thus, concern over the impact on jobs and the advantage in collective bargaining is relatively minor compared to that in the traditional manufacturing industries.[11]

The emphasis on manufacturing employment provided by MNEs may also be connected in part with some evidence that, contrary to domestic labour market trends of ever-lower shares in manufacturing and ever-higher relative employment share in services, the relative importance of foreign manufacturing in international business operations has been increasing over the years. Thus, to use the

United States as an example, in 1970 the book value of all
American direct investment abroad was $78,100 million, of which
41.3 per cent was in manufacturing. However, according to the
census of 298 large US-based MNEs conducted by the US Department
of Commerce, manufacturing subsidiaries of American enterprises
accounted for 73 per cent of total employment by all such
subsidiaries in 1970, which was up from 71 per cent in 1966.
Manufacturing employment by US firms abroad is proportionately
higher than their share of manufacturing in assets, therefore, and
the relative importance of manufacturing operations has increased
in the post-war period.[12] Newer data shows that the value of US
investment abroad had increased to $168,000 million by 1978 of
which manufacturing accounted for 44 per cent.

     For these reasons of data availability and also particular
interest in the manufacturing industries the present report
focusses primarily on MNE employment in this sector.

Employment in foreign-owned
subsidiaries of MNEs

     A relatively substantial body of information now exists on
employment in foreign-owned as well as domestic MNEs in the main
industrialised countries as a result of OECD and EEC statistics,
government responses to the before-mentioned ILO survey, component
studies[13] prepared for the present ILO research, as well as an
increasing number of other published materials.[14] Data on employment, sales, value added, wages and salary and investment shares of
foreign-owned manufacturing enterprises in 20 industrialised market
economy countries are found in table I.3. They are based on OECD
figures prepared in 1976 (for 1972-73) and updated in 1978 (to
1975-76) and supplemented by information from other sources as
indicated.[15]

     More detailed information on the relative importance of
foreign-owned MNEs (and in part the total MNE phenomenon) in the
context of individual countries, received for the present study
from governments and sometimes trade unions, employers' organisations and other sources, are presented in the following pages.[16]
Since many data so received are more recent than other available
survey results, they are summarised in table I.4 (despite obvious
differences in definitions) as an easy reference to presently
prevailing orders of magnitude.

AUSTRALIA

     In 1972-73 there were 2,076 foreign-controlled establishments
(i.e. involving, at least, 25 per cent direct foreign ownership of
voting shares of the enterprise) in the manufacturing sector, with
349,000 employees (or 27 per cent of total employment in the manufacturing industry).[17] In the same period 82, out of the 200
largest enterprise groups, which operated 929 establishments and
employed 232,947 people, were foreign-controlled. In 1975-76, of
the 200 largest enterprises, 80 were foreign-controlled, operating
845 establishments and employing 211,560 persons. This corresponded
to 17 per cent of total industrial employment in the manufacturing
sector.

Table I.3: Percentage share of foreign-owned enterprises in the manufacturing sector of principal industrialised host countries

Foreign enterprises in	Year	Employment	Sales	Value added	Wages and Salaries	Investment or gross capital formation
AUSTRALIA	1972/73	23.6	28.7	34.3	31.3	42.0
AUSTRIA	1973	20.1	22.1	22.5	21.9	20.4
BELGIUM	1968	18.3	33.0	22-29	...	...
	1975	33.0	44.0	...	...	...
	1978	38.0	...	...	...	...
CANADA	1972	43.1	51.1	...	...	...
	1974	43.1	56.2	51.0	46.1	45.1
	1975	...	...	...	...	...
DENMARK	1971	...	8.0	...	...	5.0
FINLAND	1972	2.8	...	...	...	...
	1976	3.2	2.7	3.5	...	...
FRANCE	1973	18.0	25.8	...	...	24.1
	1975	19.0	27.8	24.5	21.6	28.7
GERMANY (FED. REP.)	1972	22.4	25.1	...	...	...
ITALY	1975	25.7	...	...	...	...
JAPAN	1972	1.9	3.8	...	...	...
	1975	1.8	5.1	...	...	...
LUXEMBOURG	1972	38.0	...	...	...	...
NETHERLANDS	1971	...	19.0	...	...	...

	Year					
NEW ZEALAND	1969/70	...	33.0	...	...	...
	1973/74	8.4	...	...	...	...
NORWAY	1974	7.8	12.9	11.0	8.6	7.0
	1975	7.2	...	...	...	9.2
	1976	7.2	10.8	...	...	...
PORTUGAL	1975	7.0	9.6	...	...	...
SPAIN	1971	...	11.2	...	...	...
SWEDEN	1970	4.1	...	...	...	...
	1974	4.8	...	...	...	...
	1975	5.7	6.8	...	...	...
	1976	...	...	6.5	6.3	3.0
TURKEY	1968	4.2	7.6	...	...	...
UNITED KINGDOM	1971	10.3	14.2	13.3	...	16.2
	1973	10.8	15.3	14.7	12.5	15.8
	1975	12.4	18.7	...	...	...
UNITED STATES	1974	5.4	...	...	...	...

Sources: OECD: Penetration of multinational enterprises in manufacturing industry in member countries, op. cit., pp. 11 and 16; and Statistics updated at the end of 1978, op. cit., p.3. D. Van Den Bulcke: De multinationale ondernemeing (Ghent, 1975), p. 56 and estimate made by the author for 1978. C. Hernandez et al: Les participations étrangères dans l'industrie française au ler janvier 1972, Statistiques et études financières, septembre 1975. For Italy, New Zealand and Luxembourg, as well as 1970 data for Sweden: Government memoranda to the ILO.

Note: "Foreign-owned" is defined, according to the OECD, as referring to enterprises for which foreign ownership exceeds 50 per cent except in the cases of the United States, Japan and France for which the cut off percentage was taken as 20 per cent and Belgium 10 per cent, whereas for Italy, New Zealand and the Federal Republic of Germany it was not given. The United States figure is aggregated from sectoral data found on page 7 of the OECD updated 1978 tables.

... = Not available

AUSTRIA

Whereas there were only 237 foreign-controlled companies in Austria in 1961, their number had gone up to 3,882 by 1969. Over the same period the nominal value of foreign participation in the Austrian economy rose from 4,250 million to 10,320 million Schillings. By 1971 this figure had reached 15,310 million Schillings. In 1971 some 216,551 persons (12 per cent of all employees) worked in enterprises with majority or minority foreign participation. In the manufacturing industry alone, in that same year, 137,700 persons were employed in enterprises with majority or minority foreign participation (i.e. 22 per cent of all manufacturing employment).[18]

Using a broad concept of foreign control (i.e. a minimum of 5 per cent of foreign shareholding) the Austrian Central Statistical Office concluded that in 1971/73 1,044 enterprises were under some form of foreign influence. Still, this represented only about one per cent of the 107,858 enterprises surveyed. However, the foreign-influenced enterprises employed 183,245 persons, or 13.6 per cent of all those covered by the survey.

At the end of 1975 it was estimated that 420,000 employees were working in some 3,500 foreign-controlled enterprises in the entire economy (i.e. 20.9 per cent), whereas by 1979 this employment share was estimated at 25 per cent approximately. For the manufacturing industry alone in 1975 the employment share of foreign-controlled enterprises was about 30 per cent.

BELGIUM

In 1975, foreign-controlled firms employed some 311,000 persons in the Belgian manufacturing industry.[19] From 1968-75 a decline occurred in total manufacturing employment in Belgium. During the same period, the relative share of foreign subsidiaries in employment rose from 18 to 33 per cent. (The share of foreign-owned enterprises in employment was estimated by the authors of the Belgian component study to have risen to 38 per cent in 1978.) Start-ups by foreign firms accounted for almost 72,000 employees by 1975 (an increase of 59 per cent over 1968 levels), net of dismissals and closures. In the case of foreign acquisitions, the net addition to employment was considerably less (namely 7,300) but still positive. A certain proportion of the approximately 64,000 jobs "switched" by acquisition from Belgian to foreign-owned firms might well consist of jobs "saved" from failing companies and could thus be added to net, positive employment change. The available (fragmentary) evidence suggests, however, that the employment expansion of foreign affiliates could not be maintained during 1975/78. (See also table I.5 summarising these findings of the Belgian study.)

CANADA

A Statistics Canada publication[20] provides some recent data on the number of Canadian employees in foreign-controlled[21] establishments. Thus, in 1974, of the 1,946,043 employees in the logging, mining and manufacturing industries, 836,455 (43 per cent) worked in foreign-controlled companies; 769,946 of them were in foreign-controlled manufacturing enterprises representing 40 per cent of Canadian employment in manufacturing.

FINLAND

In 1974, foreign enterprises operating in Finland (where foreign shareholders had more than 20 per cent of the share capital) employed directly about 37,200 workers, according to the register of enterprises kept by the Statistical Centre. This percentage corresponded to between 4 and 5 per cent of the employment in the various industrial branches and to about 1.7 per cent of the total employment in Finland (the number of such foreign enterprises was 500 in 1974; for 1979 their number was estimated at 800-900). In 1976, foreign manufacturing enterprises in Finland employed 21,700 workers. The manufacturing enterprises with a foreign share capital of more than 50 per cent alone employed 16,400 workers, which corresponded to about 3.3 per cent of the total employment in the manufacturing industry.

FRANCE

As of 1 January 1973 firms with at least 20 per cent of foreign ownership accounted for 18 per cent of the 4,684,000 employees in the manufacturing industry in France. Nearly 14 per cent (647,000) were in enterprises with over 50 per cent foreign capital participation and 4.2 per cent (199,000) in firms with between 20 and 50 per cent.[22]

FEDERAL REPUBLIC OF GERMANY

The 34 largest foreign-controlled MNEs, used in a sample survey undertaken for 1974, employed 473,500 persons as against 1,459,000 who worked for the 30 largest German-owned multinationals. Although the foreign-controlled MNEs appear thus, at first sight, to be somewhat dwarfed by their German counterparts with respect to their employment figures, it has been estimated that, if the smaller foreign multinationals were also included, the total direct employment in foreign-owned manufacturing MNEs might well be in the order of 1.2 million (i.e. 15 per cent of the entire manufacturing employment in the Federal Republic).[23]

Applying data published by the German Federal Bank for 1972 a much higher estimate, of some 2,195,600 persons, is reached if all enterprises with foreign capital participation are included, irrespective of size or the actual participation percentage. This corresponds to 13.3 per cent of the total employee figure of 16,532,200.[24] However, if comparable figures with respect to size of the enterprises were used it would still be clear that MNE employment in the Federal Republic of Germany is overwhelmingly in German-owned multinationals.

ITALY

In 1975, 770,000 of the 6 million employed in the manufacturing industry in Italy were working in enterprises with foreign capital participation (12.8 per cent).

JAPAN

The number of employees in foreign-affiliated firms in Japan is obtained through an annual survey undertaken by the Ministry of International Trade and Industry since 1967. The eleventh such survey, carried out in March 1977, which addressed itself to 2,050 foreign firms (defined as those with a foreign investment ratio of 25 per cent or more) indicated that 229,000 persons were employed by the 1,101 firms (including the largest ones) replying to the questionnaire. This represented 0.9 per cent of total industrial employment in Japan. Foreign enterprises in the manufacturing industry alone employed 200,000 or 1.9 per cent (see Table I.3 and also Annex table III for further details).

LUXEMBOURG

Ten thousand persons were employed in foreign-controlled firms which represented 38 per cent of total employment in the manufacturing industry. In 1963 this figure was 2,190. This amounts to an average increase of 865 employees per year in foreign-controlled companies.[25]

NEW ZEALAND

For 1973-74 it was estimated that 138,800 or 8.43 per cent of the employees were found in companies with foreign affiliations.[26]

NORWAY

In 1976 there were 199 enterprises in Norway whose share capital was at least 50 per cent foreign. These enterprises employed 27,280 persons, or 7 per cent of the total enterprise employment.

SWEDEN

Employment in foreign majority-owned enterprises in Sweden, in 1975/76, totalled approximately 100,000. This represented 4.9 per cent of all persons gainfully employed in the country (the figure was 7.6 per cent if companies which were at least 20 per cent foreign-owned were included).[27] For the manufacturing industry alone the corresponding figure was 5.7 per cent (53,311 employees).

TURKEY

The number of employees in multinational enterprises operating under the Foreign Capital Encouragement Act in Turkey was 46,802 in 1976.

UNITED KINGDOM

According to the 1975 census of production, there were 1,030 foreign-controlled enterprises, operating 2,121 manufacturing establishments in the United Kingdom and employing 925,700 people. For the purposes of the census, the term "foreign-controlled" was applied to enterprises with a foreign equity holding of 50 per cent or more. The data collected indicated that foreign-controlled firms employed 13 per cent of the workforce in manufacturing outside the public sector and accounted for over 16 per cent of the gross value added and nearly 20 per cent of the gross output.[28]

Table I.4: Employment in manufacturing MNEs in home and host country operations 1975/77 (in thousands)*

Country	Year	Foreign-based MNEs operating in the country	Country-based MNEs	
			At home	Abroad
AUSTRALIA[1]	1975/76	211	329	...
AUSTRIA[1]	1975	153	...	...
BELGIUM[2]	1975	331	163	182
CANADA[1]	1974	770	540	360
FINLAND[1]	1976	16	20	17
FRANCE[1]	1973	647	...	...
GERMANY (FED.REP.)[2]	1974	473	1 459	556
ITALY[1]	1975	770	...	357
JAPAN[1]	1977	200	...	654
LUXEMBOURG[1]	1972	10	...	...
NETHERLANDS[3]	1975/77	177	362[4]	1 011[4]
NEW ZEALAND	1973/74	138	...	...
NORWAY[1]	1976	27	...	...
PORTUGAL[3]	1975	44	...	...
SWEDEN[1]	1976	100	316[5]	274[5]
SWITZERLAND[6]	1974	...	214	460
TURKEY[1]	1976	46	...	...
UNITED KINGDOM[2]	1975	926	2 527	1 000
UNITED STATES[3]	1968/74	644	6 700[7]	3 301[8]

*Because of differences in scope and definition of enterprises tables 1.4 and 1.2 are not comparable.

... = not available.

Sources: Table compiled from the following sources, which are not always fully comparable and some of which provide estimates. Usually, the data are derived from samples of major enterprises.

[1] Government memoranda in reply to ILO survey for this project.

[2] Component studies for this research project (listed in Appendix).

[3] OECD (basic source Penetration by multinational enterprises, op.cit.)

[4] Ministry of Economic Affairs: Multinational enterprises: survey on a number of Dutch-based multinational enterprises by the Netherlands government (Oct. 1976), data is for 37 enterprises.

[5] Swedish Trade Union (LO) data attached to government reply to ILO survey for this project; data for 22 enterprises.

[6] Jürg Niehans: "Benefits of multinational firms for a small parent economy: the case of Switzerland", in Tamir Agmon and Charles Kindleberger: Multinationals from small countries (Cambridge, Mass., 1977), p. 6.

[7] Harvard Business School, Multinational Enterprises Project. Data for 187 largest US enterprises with manufacturing subsidiaries in six or more foreign countries.

[8] J. Curhan, Wm. Davidson and R. Suri: Tracing the multinationals: a sourcebook on US-based enterprises (Cambridge, Mass., 1977), p. 259 (data for 1975).

UNITED STATES OF AMERICA

Two estimates give indications of employment in foreign-owned MNEs in the United States. A US Department of Commerce survey[29] in 1974 placed at somewhat over 1 million the number of employees in all industries in which foreign multinationals were found with slightly more than 550,000 in manufacturing. OECD data for the same year estimated approximately 640,000 employees to be in foreign-controlled manufacturing enterprises.[30] Based on the increase in foreign investment between 1974 and 1978 it has been projected that the figure may have risen to approximately 1,670,000 by 1978.[31]

A rapid expansion of foreign enterprise employment occurred in the 1950s and 1960s in most countries (and especially in those European countries grouped in the EEC and EFTA). This inference can be drawn from earlier studies, most of which refer to foreign investment and MNE activity of US companies.[32] A vast expansion of European-based MNEs also took place during the 1960s and early 1970s in industrialised countries of Europe, especially in the then six-member European Economic Community.[33] Similarly, the government replies to the ILO survey, especially those of Australia, Austria, Luxembourg and Sweden, refer to large increases in numbers of persons employed in foreign manufacturing subsidiaries of MNEs during the 1960s, both absolutely and as a proportion of total industrial employment.[34] In summary, the following conclusions can be drawn from the available data:

(1) In the mid-1970s employment in foreign subsidiaries as a proportion of manufacturing employment varied widely among the major industrialised market economy countries, ranging from a low of less than 2 per cent in Japan to over 40 per cent in Belgium (1978) and in Canada.

(2) Foreign enterprises employed one-fifth or more of those working in manufacturing in at least seven of the major industrialised market economy countries.

(3) In several countries for which data are available for different years, notably Belgium, France, Sweden, Finland and the United Kingdom, the proportion of the total manufacturing workforce employed in foreign-owned MNE subsidiaires also visibly increased during the early 1970s (i.e. not only during the 1950s and 1960s, which was the general trend).

(4) It is noteworthy that in virtually every country for which economic indicators are available, the weight of foreign-owned enterprises in terms of manufacturing sales, value-added, wages and salaries paid, and total investment or gross capital formation, is greater than in terms of employment (see table I.3). These differentials are by and large consistent with the distinctive sectoral concentrations, skill mixes and capital and know-how intensities of MNE operations discussed later in Chapter III of this report.

Table I.5: Employment effects of foreign-owned MNEs in Belgian industry, 1968-1975

	NEW ESTABLISHMENTS		ACQUISITIONS		TOTAL	
	Change 1968-75		Change 1968-75		Change 1968-75	
	('000)	(%)	('000)	(%)	('000)	(%)
A. EMPLOYMENT CREATION	+ 93.4	+ 77	+ 19.0	+ 28	+ 112.3	+ 59
B. EMPLOYMENT LOSS	- 21.7	- 18	- 11.7	- 17	- 33.4	- 18
C. NET EMPLOYMENT EFFECTS (A-B)	+ 71.7	+ 59	+ 7.3	+ 11	+ 78.9	+ 42
D. EMPLOYMENT SWITCHES (by take-overs by Belgian enterprises of foreign affiliates, or by MNE's of Belgian companies during period)	- 3.9	- 3	+ 56.8	+ 83	+ 52.8	+ 28
E. GROSS EMPLOYMENT EFFECTS (C-D)	+ 67.7	+ 56	+ 64.1	+ 93	+ 131.8	+ 70

Source: Abridged from the Belgian component study for this project, D. Van Den Bulcke and E. Halsberghe, op. cit., table 2.1, p. 65. Columns may not add due to rounding.

It is to be noted, however, that in most countries it is not known precisely to what extent the absolute and relative increases in industrial employment in foreign enterprise subsidiaries occurred in new, "green-field" start-ups, or resulted from acqusitions or takeovers (and the same applies to domestic MNEs). The starting up of new factories and facilities by foreign (as well as domestic) MNEs are generally thought to generate considerable numbers of new employment opportunities.[35] Foreign acquisitions (as well as those by domestic MNEs), on the other hand, are sometimes a cause of concern on the grounds that in some cases such takeovers and mergers are followed by rationalisation processes which could result in a reduction rather than an increase of jobs.[36] While the Canadian experience tends to show that, in many cases, acquisitions can also be beneficial in terms of employment[37], reliable information on this question is not available for most of the other industrialised market economy countries (the Belgian component study[38] provides some detailed indications limited to that country).

It can be assumed, generally, that during the period of greatest MNE expansion (1950s, 1960s) a major proportion of the increase in employment in both foreign and domestic MNEs was due to new investments and not acquisitions.

Employment in MNEs in their home countries

All industrialised countries are to some extent both home and host countries to MNEs. The United States remains the home country of the largest amount of foreign direct investment and the largest absolute number of MNEs, although there has been an extremely rapid increase in the number of European- and Japanese-based firms with numerous foreign manufacturing subsidiaries during the past decade and a half.[39] The United Kingdom is the second most important home country of MNEs, but the proportion of their MNEs, like that of US MNEs, has gradually decreased relatively to those from Switzerland, Japan and the Federal Republic of Germany, which are also particularly important as MNEs' home countries and from the 1970s the direct foreign investment of firms based in them has taken an increasing share (see table I.6).

Due to certain limitations and lack of comparability of data, attempts to indicate the importance of MNE activity to home countries have usually been limited to comparisons of outward foreign direct investment in absolute terms or their relation to the gross domestic production. Comparisons of that type are presented in tables I.6 and I.7, partly because they remain the only readily available indicators of the relative importance of MNEs to the home economies of certain countries, such as France, Italy and Japan. Table I.7 suggests that outward MNE activity is particularly important relative to the domestic economy for Switzerland, the United Kingdom, the Netherlands, the United States and Sweden, with Canada and Belgium following close behind.

Estimates for employment in MNEs in their home countries are more scarce. Several such estimates were submitted specifically for the present study[40] and have been summarised in table I.8 so as to provide an easy reference to orders of magnitude (although the data may not be fully comparable from one country to the other). Some further details for certain countries are given hereafter.[41]

Table I.6: <u>Stock of foreign direct investment of developed market economies</u>

	1,000 MILLIONS OF DOLLARS			PERCENTAGES		
	1967	1971	1976	1967	1971	1976
UNITED STATES	57	83	137	54	52	48
UNITED KINGDOM	18	24	32	17	15	11
GERMANY (FED.REP.)	3	7	20	3	5	7
JAPAN	2	5	19	1	3	7
SWITZERLAND	5	10	19	6	6	7
FRANCE	6	7	12	6	5	4
CANADA	4	7	11	4	4	4
NETHERLANDS	2	4	10	2	3	3
SWEDEN	2	2	5	2	2	2
BELGIUM-LUXEMBOURG	2	2	4	2	2	1
ITALY	2	3	3	2	2	1
TOTAL ABOVE	103	154	272	98	99	95
ALL OTHER (ESTIMATE)	4	5	17	4	3	6
GRAND TOTAL	107	159	289	100	100	100

Source: United Nations: <u>Transnational corporations in world development: A re-examination</u> (New York, 1978; Sales No: E.78.II.A.5), p. 236. Columns may not add due to rounding.

Table I.7: Relative importance of MNE foreign direct
investment as compared to home country economies

	Outward foreign direct investment as a percentage of GDP, 1976
Belgium	5.4
Canada	5.7
France	3.4
Germany (Fed. Rep. of)	4.5
Italy	1.7
Japan	3.5
Netherlands	10.9
Sweden	6.7
Switzerland	33.2
United Kingdom	14.7
United States	8.1

Source: Calculation by G.L. Jordan and
J.-E. Vahlne in the Swedish component
study for the project, p.2 (cited in
footnote 13 to this chapter and listed
in the appendix to the study) based on
data contained in UN: Transnational
corporations in world development: A
re-examination, op. cit.

According to Statistics Canada, the 25 largest Canadian MNEs employed approximately 540,000 persons in Canada in 1975, accounting for about 6 per cent of total employment or some 29 per cent of employees in manufacturing. The large-firm survey carried out by the Canadian Department of Industry, Trade and Commerce estimated at 415,000 for 1976 and 404,000 for 1977 the total number of Canadian employees in 28 Canadian-based and controlled MNEs (the discrepancy between both years is attributable to statistical error margins rather than to a real drop in employment). Thus Canada, usually simply thought of as a host country for MNEs has nearly a third of its manufacturing employment in domestic MNEs. (Almost three-quarters of Canadian industrial employment appears to be in home and host MNEs combined.)

Seventeen thousand one hundred workers, that is 3.5 per cent of the total employment in the Finnish industry, were found in multi-national manufacturing enterprises in which Finnish citizens had majority shares.

Most of the big Swedish industrial enterprises are multinational in the sense that they own one or several manufacturing
units abroad. Using this broad definition, more than half of the
total employment in Swedish industry is now found in Swedish multinational enterprises. Although the last decade has witnessed a
strong relative increase in both Swedish direct investments abroad
and foreign direct investments in Sweden, it is, by and large,
more a home country for multinational enterprises than a host
country. According to a study by the Swedish trade unions[42] the
22 biggest Swedish-owned multinational companies employed about
254,000 persons in Sweden in 1971. By 1976 the figure had increased
to 316,000 employees. However, according to the same source, most
of this employment increase was a result of acquisitions and did
not constitute new jobs.[43]

The available information suggests further that a third or
more of manufacturing employment in the United States, Switzerland,
the Netherlands and the United Kingdom is in the home country
operations of MNEs.[44] In Belgium, which is also a major MNE host
country, nearly half the number of those employed by foreign
subsidiaries are nevertheless employed in domestic operations of
Belgian MNEs. Employment in the top two German MNEs is very nearly
equal to the combined employment in all foreign MNE subsidiaries
in the Federal Republic of Germany.[45] Exact statistics are not
available for Luxembourg, but the government reply to the ILO
survey suggests that the bulk of manufacturing employment not
covered by the 38 per cent of the industrial workforce employed by
foreign MNEs is accounted for by one large Luxembourg-headquartered
MNE; which means that in this small country nearly 100 per cent
of manufacturing employment is in MNEs.

Changes in MNE employment in home countries

Information on changes in home country MNE employment over a
period of years is fragmentary but data for the Federal Republic of
Germany, Sweden and the United Kingdom suggest that, at least in
these countries, such employment has been growing both absolutely
and relatively to total manufacturing employment in recent years.[46]
The extent to which such growth in home country MNE employment was
the result of acquisitions or of new investments is not clear in
most cases, an information gap which, as already mentioned, also
exists for the foreign-based MNEs.

At this stage, some general observations on the employment
effect of MNE new investments or acquisitions may be useful. It is
often assumed, with some justification, that new investments and
start-ups create more new job opportunities, in net terms than
acquisitions. However, especially in periods of full or overfull
employment which prevailed in many industrialised countries in the
early 1970s, one cannot exclude the hypothesis that, had multinationals failed to invest, domestic multinational enterprises would
have done so in their place. On the other hand, it can be argued
that the net employment effect of certain MNE acquisitions, even
those which result in some job-suppressing rationalisation, can be
positive in the over-all employment picture where the firms acquired
might otherwise have been obliged either to reduce employment even
more or to shut down; and that rationalisation measures can be
followed, as past experience has shown in some cases, by long-run
growth.[47] These considerations suggest in particular that the
question of acquisitions, their motives and their employment
effects, needs to be studied in much more detail than is possible
in most cases with the presently available information; and that
a short-run evaluation is not sufficient.

Table I.8: Home country employment in
multinational manufacturing enterprises

Country	Year	Employment ('000)	Percentage of total employment in manufacturing
BELGIUM	1975	163	14
CANADA	1975	540	29
GERMANY (FED.REP.)	1974	1 459	16
NETHERLANDS	1974	362	33
SWEDEN	1971	254	27
	1976	316	34
SWITZERLAND	1974	214	26
UNITED KINGDOM	1971	2 445	30
	1975	2 527	33
UNITED STATES	1968	6 700	35

Sources:

Belgium:	D. Van Den Bulcke and E. Halsberghe: Belgian component study for this research project, op. cit.
Canada:	Statistics Canada study noted by the Canadian Government memorandum prepared for the ILO survey.
Germany (F.R.):	Rolf Jungnickel, Henry Krägenau, Mattheas Lefeldt, Manfred Holthus, Barbara Erhardt: Einfluss multinationaler Unternehmen auf Aussenwirtschaft und Branchenstruktur der Bundesrepublik Deutschland (Hamburg, HWWA-Institut, 1977), pp. 40-41, referred to in the component study for the Federal Republic of Germany.
Netherlands:	Ministry of Economic Affairs: Multinational enterprises: survey on a number of Dutch-based multinational enterprises by the Netherlands government, op. cit.
Switzerland:	Jürg Niehans: "Benefits of multinational firms for a small parent economy: the case of Switzerland", in Agmon, op. cit.
Sweden:	Swedish Trade Union (LO) estimates submitted by the government in connection with the ILO survey. Figures are for the "22 largest Swedish-owned MNEs".
United Kingdom:	John Stopford: UK component study, op. cit. Data for the 118 UK industrial firms among the largest 250 as of 1978 which had three or more overseas manufacturing facilities.
United States:	Harvard Business School, Multinational Enterprise Project. Data for 187 largest US enterprises with manufacturing subsidiaries in six or more foreign countries.

It should be noted that the sources used are not always fully comparable and that some of them provide estimates. Usually, the data are derived from samples of major enterprises.

MNE employment abroad

It is especially thanks to the memoranda received from governments for this study that some information can be given regarding this question with respect to the following countries.[48]

CANADA

Between 1960 and 1974, Canadian MNE direct investment abroad almost quadrupled and, by 1974, 76 per cent of such investment was in other industrialised countries. From this one can assume that the growth in employment abroad of Canadian MNEs has probably been greater than in the home country.

In 1975, 360,000 of the 900,000 persons employed by the 25 largest Canadian-based MNEs were working in subsidiaries abroad.

FINLAND

In 1977, the Bank of Finland carried out an investigation on the foreign subsidiaries of Finnish multinationals. It was found that these subsidiaries employed 206,600 workers (subsidiaries being defined as enterprises with a capital participation of Finnish firms of at least 20 per cent).

FEDERAL REPUBLIC OF GERMANY

A survey of 11 major German MNEs in the Federal Republic, for which adequate data were available for 1966, showed that 13.6 per cent of their workforce was employed outside the country. However, figures for 1971 indicated that the 33 leading German-owned and headquartered MNEs, had already 22.2 per cent of their total workforce abroad (i.e. 418,700 persons out of a total of 1,886,000). Using a broader enterprise sample, including also the smaller multinationals, it was estimated that the total number employed overseas in 1971 by German multinationals was in the neighbourhood of 600,000.[49]

By 1974, the top 30 German-owned MNEs had 28 per cent of their total workforce abroad, i.e. 556,000 out of some 2,015,000 workers. Virtually the same percentage of foreign employment in German multinationals was obtained in that year by a study covering a larger sample of 149 German multinationals[50] (336,151 persons in foreign operations out of a total employment of 1,516,379 in German-owned MNEs). There is little doubt that employment in foreign subsidiaries of German-owned MNEs has increased in the 1970s to a considerably greater extent than domestic employment in these enterprises. From the relatively similar samples of enterprises used for the benchmark calculations of 1971 and 1974, it can be assumed that foreign employment of the largest German MNEs during these three years rose by more than 30 per cent (137,300 persons), while their domestic employment level increased by 7 per cent (128,700 persons). Thus, in absolute terms, for every additional domestic employment unit, 1.1 employment units were added to the foreign labour force.[51]

ITALY

For 1974, employment abroad of Italian MNEs was as follows: 208,000 (58 per cent) in OECD countries; 149,000 (42 per cent) in other countries. Thirty per cent (113,000) of the total foreign employment of Italian MNEs was in Latin America.

JAPAN

The number of overseas employees of Japanese enterprises (i.e. of those which are more than 25 per cent owned or with which a permanent economic relationship exists) is established through annual surveys of the Japanese Ministry of International Trade and Industry (referred to before). The sixth survey of March 1976 to which 1,584 out of 3,119 "head office" companies replied, showed that 653,800 persons were employed abroad by these enterprises, 10,800 of which were Japanese. The manufacturing enterprises alone employed 556,000 persons abroad. For further details see Annex table IV to this chapter.

SWEDEN

Between 1965 and 1974, the total number of employees in foreign sales and production subsidiaries - majority-owned by Swedish manufacturing corporations - increased to about 300,000 persons, corresponding to a 50 per cent increase. (Over the same period, employment in Swedish industry as a whole registered a small decrease. However, because of the complex economic inter-relationships involved, both trends cannot be simply correlated.) The regional distribution of employment in foreign production subsidiaries of Swedish MNEs over the years is given in the following table:

Table I.9: Percentage number of employees in foreign production subsidiaries of Swedish enterprises, distributed by region

Region	1960	1965	1970	1974
Nordic countries	7	8	10	9
EFTA (including Great Britain and Denmark)	14	12	12	11
EEC (excluding Great Britain and Denmark)	46	47	46	44
Rest of Europe	1	1	1	3
North America	12	10	7	8
Australia, New Zealand, Africa and Japan	3	4	4	4
Latin America	7	9	12	14
Other countries	10	9	8	7
	100	100	100	100

Source: Swedish Government reply to ILO survey.

The table shows the importance of the six original EEC countries as host countries for Swedish direct investments. The most marked changes are a strong relative increase in Latin America and a relative decrease in North America (mainly the United States).

UNITED KINGDOM

According to the United Kingdom component study[52], the 118 major UK-based MNEs increased their workforce in foreign operations by approximately 150,000 to 1 million during the four years 1971-75. At the same time their domestic employment increase in the United Kingdom was about 80,000. As indicated before, a large proportion of these jobs were added by acquisitions.

SWITZERLAND

Data collected for a survey conducted for the present project[53] indicate that some 72,493 persons were working in Swiss MNEs in 40 developing countries in 1977, representing an increase of 53,146 in 17 years according to a recent article.[54] The article analysing the survey results noted at the same time that employment by these MNEs in Switzerland itself also increased during this period. An earlier academic study had estimated that the 35 largest Swiss MNEs employed a total of some 460,400 persons in all host countries in 1974.[55]

Evolution of MNE employment abroad and at home

The data reviewed in the previous section together with the information collected through the ILO study on MNE employment trends in 40 developing countries[56] and information obtained from other sources[57] suggest that, generally speaking, the employment provided by Australian, European, Japanese and American-based MNEs in foreign countries (especially the developing countries) during the last 10 to 15 years has expanded faster than their home country employment.[58]

Notes

[1] As reported in Lawrence G. Franko: Multinational enterprises, the international division of labour in manufactures and the developing countries (Geneva, ILO, 1975; mimeographed World Employment Programme research working paper; restricted distribution).

[2] Commission of the European Communities: Survey of multinational enterprises, Vol. I (Brussels, 1976), p. 33 (see tables 1.1 and 1.2 of this chapter).

[3] An earlier study, ILO: The impact of multinational enterprises on employment and training (Geneva 1976) referred to employment estimates provided in the United Nations report : Multinational corporations and world development (New York, 1975). The UN placed employment in foreign subsidiaries in all market economy countries in 1970 at some 13 to 14 million. According to the ILO study, 2 million of these were, at the time, considered to be in developing countries. The world-wide Harvard and EEC employment

estimates quoted in the present report have a different scope.
They relate not only to employees in multinational enterprises in
host countries but also include employment provided by MNEs in
their home countries.

[4] Details on this estimate, based on a vareity of recent
surveys and proxy indicators, are given in the companion report
to this study, ILO: Employment effects of multinational enterprises in developing countries (Geneva, forthcoming 1981).

[5] It must be admitted, however, that this is a very
approximate figure since no detailed data exist to support this
estimate.

[6] Organisation for Economic Co-operation and Development
(OECD): Penetration of multinational enterprises in manufacturing
industry in member countries (Paris, 1977), and Penetration of
multinational enterprises in manufacturing industry in member
countries: Statistics updated at end of 1978 (Paris, 1979).

[7] In support of the present study, the ILO undertook in
1978/79 an inquiry among the labour ministries of 26 industrialised
market economy countries based on a catalogue of points of interest.
Fifteen comprehensive country replies were received in the form of
special memoranda from Australia, Austria, Canada, Finland, France,
the Federal Republic of Germany, Italy, Japan, Luxembourg, the
Netherlands, New Zealand, Norway, Portugal, Sweden and Turkey.
The reports contain statistics as well as other government state-
ments and evaluations.

[8] OECD: Economic outlook (Paris, July 1979).

[9] For a survey of recent United States' experience, see David
Birch: The job generation process (Cambridge, Mass., MIT Program
on Neighbourhood and Regional Change, 1979).

[10] The Canadian Government memorandum in response to the ILO
inquiry (mentioned in footnote 7) refers, in this context, to a
study by the Canadian Federation of Independent Business (based on
Statistics Canada data) which stressed the role of small business
in job generation in recent years. The study found that whereas
27 per cent of the new jobs offered in the total private sector
from 1961-71 was by firms with less than 20 employees, this percentage had increased to 50 per cent for the period 1971-77 and was
97 per cent between 1976 and 1977. These small enterprises were
rarely MNEs, although instances certainly exist of relatively small
firms already having foreign subsidiaries or "multinationalising"
because of the nature of their products or services.

[11] Robert G. Hawkins and Michael Jay Jedel: "US jobs and
foreign investment" in Duane Kujawa (ed.): International labor
and multinational enterprise (New York, Praeger, 1975), pp. 48-49.
Some services may, however, be rather mobile such as engineering
and finance. Also with regard to the location of regional
administrative headquarters much discretion seems to exist.

[12] Ibid., p. 49. See also John Fayerweather: International business strategy and administration (Cambridge, Mass., Ballinger, 1978).

[13] See the Appendix for a complete list of these working papers.

[14] Some of the more relevant recent studies are the following: Peter J. Buckley, Alan G. Hartley and John Sparkes: The employment effects of intra-EEC foreign direct investment (Brussels, Commission of the European Communities, 1980; Programme of research and action on the development of the labour market, Study No. 78/1 (V/198/80-EN)); D. Van Den Bulcke, et al.: De Multinationale Ondernemingen in de Belgische Ekonomie (Ghent, 1978); D. Van Den Bulcke, J.J. Boddewyn, B. Martens and P. Klemmer: Investment and divestment policies of multinational corporations in Europe (Westmead (UK), Saxon House, 1979); Business International: The effects of US corporate foreign investment 1970-78 (New York, Business International Corporation, 1980); H. Günter: "An overview of some recent research on multinational corporations and labour", in International Institute for Labour Studies (IILS) Bulletin, No. 12, 1974, pp. 37-46; R. Hawkins: Job displacement and the multinational firm: A methodological review (Washington, 1972; Centre for Multinational Studies; occasional paper No.3; D. Kujawa (ed): International labor and the multinational enterprise, op. cit.; S. Lall (ed.): Oxford Bulletin of Economics and Statistics, Special issue on the multinational corporation, Vol.41 (Nov. 1979) No. 4, pp. 251-388; Bruno Liebhaberg: Relations industrielles et entreprises multinationales en Europe (Paris, CEEIM, 1980); D. McAleese and D. McDonald: "Employment growth and the development of linkages in foreign-owned and domestic manufacturing enterprises", in Oxford Bulletin of Economics and Statistics, Vol.40, No. 4, 1978, pp.321-339; C.A. Michalet: The multinational companies in the new international division of labour (Geneva, ILO, 1975; mimeographed World Employment Programme research working paper; restricted distribution); Ministry of Economic Affairs: Multinational enterprises: Survey of a number of Dutch-based multinational enterprises conducted by the Netherlands Government (October 1976; mimeographed); A. Morgan and R. Blainpain: Industrial relations and the employment impacts of multinational enterprises: An inquiry into the issues (Paris, OECD, 1977); B. Stobaugh: "How investment abroad creates jobs at home", in Harvard Business Review (Boston) Sept.-Oct. 1972, pp. 118-126; Wm. H. Waldorf and V. Carlip: Transnational corporations: Their impact on labor markets, a literature survey prepared for the United Nations Centre on Transnational Corporations (New York, 1978; mimeographed); and Stephen Young and Neil Hood: "The strategies of US multinationals in Europe", in Multinational business, Economist Intelligence Unit, No. 2, 1980, pp. 1-19.

[15] In most of the sources used for the table, foreign multinationals are defined as enterprises whose foreign ownership exceeds 50 per cent except in the cases of the United States, Japan and France where the foreign ownership ratio is 20 per cent and Belgium where it is 10 per cent. In the cases of Italy and the Federal Republic of Germany the total ownership value of the enterprise covered as foreign MNEs is not given for the OECD data.

[16] Unless otherwise stated, the information given in this section is derived from the ILO survey among Governments referred to in footnote 7 above.

[17] Transnational Corporations Research Project, University of
Sydney: Transnational corporations and employment in Australia:
Some preliminary calculations (Sydney, April 1979), paper prepared
at the request of the Government of Australia for the ILO survey
mentioned in footnote 7.

[18] Multinationale Konzerne und Gewerkschaften in Österreich,
Bundeskongress des ÖGB, Wien, 15-19 September 1975, submitted as
Appendix E to the memorandum of the Austrian Government to the ILO
survey mentioned in footnote 7.

[19] D. Van Den Bulcke and E. Halsberghe, component study on
Belgium prepared for this project (see list in appendix).

[20] Statistics Canada: Domestic and foreign control of manufacturing, mining and logging establishments in Canada (Ottawa,
1974).

[21] An enterprise is considered as "foreign-controlled" if
50 per cent or more of its voting rights are known to be held
outside Canada or held by one or more Canadian corporations that
are themselves foreign-controlled.

[22] "Principaux résultats sur l'importance relative des
participations étrangères dans l'industrie française", in Les
participations étrangères dans l'industrie française, au 1er
janvier 1973, extrait de Statistiques et études financières No. 321,
sept. 1975, pp. 104-126, annexed to the government memorandum
mentioned in footnote 7.

[23] Rolf Jungnickel, Henry Krägenau, Matthias Lefeld, Manfred
Holthus and Barbara Erhardt: Einfluss multinationaler Unternehmen
auf Aussenwirtschaft und Branchenstruktur der Bundesrepublik
Deutschland (Hamburg, 1977), pp. 38-44, also mentioned in
P. Bailey, component study on the Federal Republic of Germany
prepared for the present project (cited in appendix).

[24] "Ausländische Beteiligung an Unternehmen der Bundesrepublik"
in Monatsberichte der Deutschen Bundesbank, Vol. 26, No. 11
(November 1974), pp. 28 and 30.

[25] Cf. in particular Bulletin du STATEC No. 5/1973: La
seconde révolution industrielle au Luxembourg. Un bilan
intérimaire submitted with the government's memorandum.

[26] New Zealand Department of Labour.

[27] The figures in brackets are extracted from G.L. Jordan and
J.E. Vahlne, the component study on Sweden prepared for the present
project (see appendix). In their reply contained in Summary of
reports on the effect given to the Tripartite Declaration of
Principles concerning multinational enterprises and social policy,
GB/MNE/1980/D.1 (Geneva, 22-26 October 1980), p. 29, the Swedish
government attributed the increase from 90,000 to 100,000, between
1971 and 1975, to acquisitions, a point disputed by the Swedish
Employers' Confederation since the net result in their opinion
cannot be calculated with precision, ibid., p. 30.

[28] All enterprises employing 20 or more people were covered and estimates made for smaller undertakings. The data presented here for the United Kingdom was taken from J.M. Stopford, the component study on the United Kingdom prepared for this report (cited in the appendix).

[29] D. Kujawa, US component study for this project (see list in appendix).

[30] OECD: Penetration of multinational enterprises in manufacturing industries, op. cit.

[31] Kujawa, op. cit.

[32] Notably, Raymond Vernon: Sovereignty at bay (London, 1971).

[33] See Lawrence G. Franko: The European multinationals: A renewed challenge to American and British big business (London, Harper and Row, 1976), especially Ch.VI, p. 137.

[34] See footnote 7. According to the information submitted by Australia, a common feature throughout the various industries within the manufacturing sector was that the average foreign-controlled establishment was a good deal larger than the average Australian establishment. On average, for the sector as a whole, large foreign-controlled factories tended to employ more people than Australian-controlled establishments - and the employment effects of new foreign implantation were thus particularly substantial.

For Austria, it is noted that subsidiaries made a significant contribution towards overcoming problems of structural changes and thus the maintenance of high levels of employment. For example, in the 1960s, foreign investors favoured the low-wage, economically weaker regions in Austria which also had a surplus of labour at that time.

In Luxembourg, employment in MNEs increased from 2,190 in 1963 to 9,964 by 1972.

According to the Swedish government's memorandum, the number of employees in foreign-owned companies in Sweden (i.e. companies which were at least 20 per cent foreign-owned) more than doubled between 1962 and 1975.

[35] See, for example, a French government view in Délégation à l'aménagement du territoire et à l'action régionale (DATAR): Investissements étrangers et aménagements du territoire, Livre blanc, Paris 1974.

[36] Canadian Government memorandum (see footnote 7). This concern about possible negative effects on employment from foreign acquisitions and takeovers was one factor which led the Canadian government to establish its procedures under the Foreign Investment Review Act (FIRA), for examining proposed foreign direct investments.

[37] In the 1977/78 fiscal year it was found that employment increase occurred in 141 of the 241 takeover cases and in 291 of the 300 new business cases allowed by the Foreign Investment Review Agency. Over the five-year period ending March 1979, roughly 70 per cent of the acquisitions authorised and 98 per cent of proposals to establish new businesses were judged to offer benefits in terms of employment. In all, the investment proposals accepted during this period provided directly for nearly 52,000 jobs.

[38] D. Van Den Bulcke and E. Halsberghe, op. cit.

[39] See Lawrence G. Franko: "Multinationals: The end of US dominance" in Harvard Business Review (Nov.-Dec. 1978) pp. 93-100, and The European multinationals, op. cit.; United Nations: Transnational corporations in world development: A re-examination, op. cit. and Yoshiro Tsurumi: The Japanese are coming (Cambridge, Mass., Ballinger, 1976).

[40] Through government memorandum in reply to the ILO survey mentioned in footnote 7.

[41] If not otherwise stated, the following information is derived from the memoranda mentioned in footnote 7.

[42] LOs utredningsavdelning (Sweden): Changes in employment in the 22 biggest Swedish multinational corporations. Fully comparable statistics are not, however, completely available.

[43] Ibid.

[44] See table I.9 and the sources indicated.

[45] Jungnickel, et al, op. cit., as well as Bailey, op.cit.

[46] See the respective component studies prepared for this project (listed in the appendix).

[47] This point has been made in particular in the Canadian government reply to the ILO survey mentioned before (see foonote 7).

[48] Unless otherwise indicated, the information given hereafter is derived from these memoranda.

[49] M. Holthus, R. Jungnickel, G. Koopmann, K. Matthies and R. Sutter: Die deutschen multinationalen Unternehmen: Die Internationalisierungsprozess der deutschen Industrie (Frankfurt, Athenäum Verlag, 1974), pp. 144-147.

[50] Folker Fröbel, Jürgen Heinrichs and Otto Kreye: The new international division of labour: Structural unemployment in industrialised countries and industrialisation in developing countries (Cambridge, University Press, 1980), p. 196.

[51] Component study on the Federal Republic of Germany for this project, P.J. Bailey, op. cit., p. 12.

[52] United Kingdom component study for this research project, J. Stopford, op. cit., pp. 37-38, overseas data for 77 firms.

[53] This survey investigated the trends in the employment in MNEs in the 40 most important developing countries (in terms of foreign direct investment). The results of this ILO survey, which was addressed to a sample of more than 250 MNEs in 12 home countries (in Australia, Canada, Japan and Europe), are discussed in the companion report on employment effects of MNEs in developing countries (see footnote 4).

[54] "Les effets de l'activité des multinationales dans le domaine de l'emploi", Journal des Associations patronales, No. 10, 1979, pp. 192-193.

[55] J. Niehans: "Benefits of multinational firms for a small parent economy: the case of Switzerland", in Tamir Agmon and Charles Kindleberger, Multinationals from small countries (Cambridge, Mass., 1977), p. 6.

[56] See footnote 53 above.

[57] Especially the component study to this project.

[58] According to the ILO survey mentioned in footnote 53, the employment provided by the more than 250 sample enterprises, from Australia, Canada, Japan and Europe, in 40 developing countries in Africa, Asia and Latin America increased from 1960 to 1977 by more than 150 per cent (including employment provided by new enterprises).

ANNEX Table I: Level of total employment in principal industrialised countries: selected years, 1965 through 1979 as a percentage of 1970 levels (1970 = 100)

	1965	1966	1968	1973	1975	1977	1978	1979
NORTH AMERICA AND JAPAN								
CANADA	87.1	90.8	95.7	111.4	119.4[a]	124.0	128.2	133.3
UNITED STATES	90.4	92.7	96.6	107.4	107.8	115.2	120.0	123.3
JAPAN	92.9	94.9	98.2	103.2	102.5	104.9	106.2	107.6
EUROPE								
BELGIUM	...	...	...	102.2	102.1	101.2	101.2	102.3
FRANCE	95.8	96.5	96.8	102.3	101.7	102.8	102.8	102.8
GERMANY (FED. REP.)	101.0	100.6	97.4	100.1	95.8	93.7	94.3	95.6[b]
ITALY	101.7	99.7	100.6	99.0	101.6	107.3[c]	107.8	105.6
NETHERLANDS	95.5	96.2	96.9	99.8	99.3	99.4	99.8	100.7
SWEDEN	96.0	96.9	97.0	100.7	105.4	106.4	106.8	108.4
SWITZERLAND	...	...	...	102.5	96.6	93.5	94.1	94.8
UNITED KINGDOM	102.2	102.3	100.3	100.9	100.9	100.7	100.9	101.3

SOURCE: ILO: Yearbook of Labour Statistics, 1979, table 4, p. 202 ff, and the Yearbook, 1980.

[a] Data for 1965-1973 not fully comparable with those for 1975-1979.

[b] Provisional data.

[c] Data for 1965-1975 not fully comparable with those for 1977-1979.

... = not available.

ANNEX table II: Employment in manufacturing industry
(millions of persons employed in manufacturing, 1965-1979)

	1965	1973	1974	1975	1976	1977	1978	1979	Percentage change 1973-1979
NORTH AMERICA AND JAPAN									
CANADA	1.64	1.94	1.99	1.87[a]	1.92	1.88	1.96	2.07	+ 6.7
UNITED STATES	18.06	20.08	20.05	18.32	18.98	19.68	20.48	21.0	+ 4.5
JAPAN	14.43	14.43	14.27	13.46	13.45	13.40	13.26	13.33	- 7.0
EUROPE									
BELGIUM	1.28	1.19	1.20	1.13	1.08	1.04	1.00	.97	- 18.0
FRANCE	5.57	5.90	5.96	5.78	5.72	5.70	5.60	5.50	- 7.0
GERMANY (FED.REP.)	10.14	9.54	9.41	8.89	8.78	8.76	8.74	8.81	- 8.0
ITALY	5.48	5.90	6.10	6.13	6.15	5.48[b]	5.43	...	- 8.0[c]
NETHERLANDS	1.33	1.13	1.13	1.09	1.04	1.02	...	...	- 10.0[d]
SWEDEN	1.22	1.07	1.12	1.14	1.10	1.06	1.02	1.03	- 4.0
SWITZERLAND	.88[e]	.81	.81	.72	.68	.68	.68	.68	- 16.0
UNITED KINGDOM	9.03	7.95	7.99	7.61	7.37	7.41	7.35	7.28	- 8.0

Source: ILO: Yearbook of Labour Statistics, 1980, table 3, p. 168 ff, and earlier years.

[a] Data for 1965-1973 not fully comparable with those for 1975-1979.

[b] Data for 1965-1976 not fully comparable with those for 1977-1979.

[c] Change 1973-1978.

[d] Change 1973-1977.

[e] 1966.

... = not available.

ANNEX Table III: Changes in number of employees in foreign-controlled enterprises in Japan

	4th survey June 1970	5th survey June 1971	6th survey June 1972	7th survey June 1973	8th survey June 1974	9th survey March 1975	10th survey March 1976	11th survey March 1977
Enterprises covered[1]	862	1 002	1 176	1 464	1 688	1 774	2 034	2 050
Enterprises which replied	693	750	853	1 051	955	1 112	1 023	1 101
Number of employees (thousands)								
All industries	178	199	232	239	247	235	205	229
Manufacturing	152	171	197	205	210	198	164	200
The ratio of the above employees to all employees in Japan (per cent)[2]								
All industries	-	0.6	1.1	1.1	1.1	1.1	0.8	0.9
Manufacturing	-	1.5	1.9	1.9	2.0	1.8	1.6	1.9

Source: Japanese Government reply to the ILO survey for this research.

1 In the 4th to 8th surveys, "enterprises covered" means enterprises where the ratio of foreign investment is more than 20 per cent and foreign companies have acquired stocks issued by the enterprises for the purpose of participation in management. From the 9th survey onward, the same term means enterprises where the ratio of foreign investment is 25 per cent or more. However, with regard to such restricted industries as public utilities, banking and transport, the same term means, in all the surveys, enterprises where the ratio of foreign investment is 15 per cent or more.

2 "All employees in Japan" have been quoted from the number of employees in all corporations in the "Annual Report on Corporations" compiled by the Ministry of Finance.

ANNEX Table IV: Changes in the number of employees in Japanese enterprises abroad

	1st survey Mar. 1971	2nd survey Mar. 1972	3rd survey Mar. 1973	4th survey Mar. 1974	5th survey Mar. 1975	6th survey Mar. 1976
Head office companies covered[1]	1 410	1 146	1 570	2 446	2 725	3 119
Head office companies which replied	724	610	793	1 295	1 379	1 584
Local corporations[2] which replied	1 188	1 423	1 786	2 723	3 224	3 275
Number of local corporations examined	957	1 402	1 747	2 263	3 204	3 275
Number of personnel despatched by the Japanese side	7 922	10 500	10 831	12 458	14 737	10 800
Average personnel per company	8.3	7.5	6.2	5.5	4.6	3.3
Employment of local personnel	165 000	252 000	320 000	478 000	629 000	643 000
Average personnel per company	172	172	183	209	196	197
Percentage of Japanese personnel dispatched as compared with the total number of employees in local corporations	4.8	4.1	3.4	2.6	2.3	1.7

Source: Japanese Government reply to the ILO survey for this research.

1 "Head office companies covered" means Japanese companies (excepting those engaged in banking or insurance, immovables, transport or communications, electricity, gas water steam supply) which, after obtaining permission to acquire foreign currency securities under the Foreign Exchange and Foreign Trade Control Law, participate in the management of foreign corporations (limited to those engaged in agriculture, forestry or fisheries, mining, manufacturing or commerce (excepting restaurant business)).

2 "Local corporations" mean foreign corporations which are an object of overseas direct investment by a head office company, more specifically, corporations in which the ratio of investment by the head office company is 25 per cent or more and those in which the ratio of investment by the head office company is less than 25 per cent and with which such a permanent economic relationship as the sending of executives, technical tie-up, the supply of materials, the purchase of products, etc., financial assistance or the conclusion of a general agent contract is established.

CHAPTER II

MNE EMPLOYMENT IN DIFFERENT INDUSTRIES

Sectoral distribution of MNEs

The available studies show that MNE activity is largely concentrated in certain industries and that it is considerably more important, as a proportion of total activity and employment, in some sectors of industry than in others. Although there are exceptions to the rule, MNEs have been found to constitute in industrialised market economy countries a particularly high propor- tion of undertakings in industries which make relatively intensive use of technology (as measured by research and development expendi- tures as a percentage of sales, or scientific and technical personnel as a proportion of total employment), marketing know-how (advertising and marketing expenditures as a percentage of sales revenue) and capital. Thus, in terms of sales and employment shares (see table II.1), MNEs loom large in industries such as chemicals, pharmaceuticals, petroleum refining, electrical and non-electrical machinery and transport equipment, especially automobiles and spare parts.[1] MNE activity appears less marked in non-ferrous metals and, generally, of rather small importance, in textiles and wearing apparel and in steel. Finally, there appear to be industries in which they are practically absent in most countries, such as ship- building.[2]

Detailed sector data on employment or other indicators of MNE activity (analogous to the global data presented in Chapter I) are sparse and fragmentary. Moreover, MNE sectoral trends over time are known only for a few countries. Employment percentages for foreign-owned subsidiaries in various (fairly aggregated[3]) industries and sectors in several countries (see tables II.2 and II.3) are generally consistent with the percentage of sales or concentration data for MNEs given in table II.1 in that the propor- tions involved are rather similar.

In the early or mid-1970s, more than one-fifth of employment in chemicals and pharmaceuticals, for example, was accounted for by foreign-owned subsidiaries in the Federal Republic of Germany (26.9 per cent), France (33.2 per cent), Austria (32.9 per cent), the United Kingdom (21.7 per cent), Australia (54.3 per cent) and in Canada (74.2 per cent). Much lower proportions of employment in foreign subsidiaries were found in textiles, leather and clothing (for instance, United Kingdom 2.5 per cent and France 8 per cent). Only in Australia and Canada did employment in foreign-owned MNEs in these industries exceed 15 per cent (table II.2).

The uneven distribution of MNEs in the economies of industrialised market economy countries is further illustrated by some detailed studies undertaken at the national level. Thus the sectoral breakdown of sales in domestic MNEs, foreign MNEs and other enterprises in the Federal Republic of Germany for 1973 confirms the view that MNE activities are usually concentrated in technology-intensive industries such as chemicals, electrical engineering and the automotive industry; and capital-intensive industries, such as petroleum refining (but not metallurgy). Table II.4 presents graphically the principal results of this study and shows that in 1973 MNEs, domestic and foreign, in the Federal Republic of Germany accounted for 50 per cent or more of

Table II.1: MNE presence and employment trends by industry

Industry	Percentage share of US-based MNEs in total US sales (1964)	Number of US- and continental-European-based MNEs in sector world-wide (1971)[a]	Employment trends by industry 1970-76 (1970 = 100)				
			USA	Germany (Fed.Rep.)[b]	UK	Belgium[c]	France
Chemicals							
- industrial	80	} 57	+ 0.3	- 3.1	- 7.6	+ 6.6	+ 4.3
- others, incl. pharma.	90		- 5.6	...	- 0.8	...	...
Petroleum refining	77	17	+ 8.9	- 8.8[d]	- 13.0[d]	- 14.2	- 5.7[e]
Electrical machinery	76	34	- 4.3	+ 0.6[f]	- 14.4	- 8.7	+ 5.6[e]
Non-electrical machinery	67	25	...	...	- 21.1	...	+ 5.6
Transport equipment of which	...	25	- 1.2	...	- 9.7	+ 7.3	...
- automobiles + parts	90	...	...	- 2.3[f]	...	...	+ 0.6[e]
- other	...	...	...	- 4.4[f]	...	...	+ 2.7[e]
Non-ferrous metals	62	10	- 6.1	- 22.8	- 20.9	- 3.6	+ 3.9
Textiles and wearing apparel	29	4	- 1.4	- 24.7	- 26.1	- 16.5	- 11.5
Steel	7	7	- 15.4	- 10.4[g]	- 14.1[g]	- 21.2	- 11.0[g]

Sources: Percentage share of US-based MNEs in total US sales from James W. Vaupel: Characteristics and motivations of the US corporations that venture abroad (Harvard Business School, Multinational Enterprise Project, 3 May 1971; unpublished manuscript); number of US and continental European-based MNEs, from L.G. Franko: The European multinationals, op.cit., p. 15; Employment trends by sector, from ILO: Yearbook of Labour Statistics, 1978 (Geneva 1979) except for data on petroleum refining, electrical and transport equipment in France and for electrical machinery and transportation equipment in the Federal Republic of Germany which

are taken from the Statistical Office of the European Communities (Eurostat)
Employment and unemployment 1971-1977 (Brussels, 1978) and data on the steel
industry for the Federal Republic of Germany, United Kingdom and France
which are taken from Eurostat: Iron and steel bulletin (Brussels, 1978).

a Number of "Fortune list" US- and continental European-based enterprises
   in the manufacturing industry with subsidiaries in seven or more countries.

b 1972-1976

c 1972-1975

d 1971-1975

e 1973-1976

f 1974-1977

g October 1978 as a percentage of 1973.

   ... = not available.

Table II.2: Percentage employed in enterprises or establishments with foreign participation: countries by order of rank in the manufacturing industry

International Standard Industrial Classification (ISIC)	Canada[1] 1974 a	Germany (Fed.Rep.)[2] 1972 a + b	Australia[1] 1972/3 a b	Austria[1] 1973 a
Major Division 2. Mining and Quarrying	49.0	12.5	32.1 6.4	...
Major Division 3. Manufacturing	43.1	22.4	23.6 4.9	20.7
31. Manufacture of food, beverages and tobacco	42.4	26.2	28.6	19.1
32. Textile, wearing apparel and leather industries	25.7	...	15.9	...
33. Manufacture of wood and wood products, including furniture	20.1	...	6.4	8.7
34. Manufacture of paper and paper products, printing and publishing	30.4	...	14.9	...
35. Manufacture of chemicals and chemical, petroleum coal, rubber and plastic products	74.2	26.9	54.3	32.9
36. Manufacture of non-metallic mineral products, except products of petroleum and coal	48.3	...	14.5	22.5
37. Basic metal industries	20.5	30.8	26.2	5.7
38. Manufacture of fabricated metal products, machinery and equipment	58.4	25.9	37.0	22.8
39. Other manufacturing industries	44.6	...	11.4	13.6
Major Division 6. Wholesale and retail trade, restaurants and hotels	...	6.4	...	6.7

Source: Adapted from OECD: Penetration of multinational enterprises in manufacturing industry in member countries, statistics updated at the end of 1978 (Paris, 1978).

a = Foreign participation exceeding 50 per cent.

b = Foreign participation between 20 and 50 per cent.

France[2]	United Kingdom[1]	Norway[1]		Portugal[2]		Sweden[2]		Finland[1]		Japan[2]
1975	1973	1976		1975		1975		1976		1975
a + b	a	a	b	a	b	a	b	a	b	a + b
...	...)	7.2	5.2	29.9	10.2	2.6	...	0.4	...	0.0
19.0	10.8)			7.0	5.3	5.7	2.7	3.2	1.0	1.8
...	8.2	2.8	0.2	3.8	3.3	10.1	3.9	1.7	2.2	0.6
8.0	2.5	...	...	3.1	1.8	3.8	1.1	6.6	0.3	0.2
8.8	0.9	...	...	1.9	1.8	0.5	0.3	0.2	0.0	0.0
10.7	3.4	2.2	0.7	4.9	0.4	2.2	2.2	0.5	0.0	0.6
33.2	21.7	11.1	22.9	14.5	8.8	14.5	5.5	6.5	0.8	3.8
15.5	4.5	4.0	3.1	1.4	7.1	3.6	3.2	0.9	0.5	4.3
17.3	15.7	19.3	24.4	5.8	6.4	3.0	6.3	1.1	3.5	0.1
21.6	15.9	10.7	3.2	14.3	10.8	6.3	2.2	4.1	1.6	0.2
14.9	...	...	...	11.5	5.3	8.8	1.5	9.8	...	2.4
...	...	...	...	5.8	2.4	8.5	1.0	...	...	0.3

... = not available.

[1] Data based on establishments of enterprises.

[2] Enterprise data.

NOTES FOR TABLES II.2 and II.3[*]

Federal Republic of Germany:

Category 38 includes musical instruments, sports equipment, toys and jewellery enterprises.

Category 6 excludes restaurants and hotels.

France:

The data excludes food industries, man-made fibres and the aeronautical industry but includes natural gas.

United Kingdom:

Rubber is included under "others" (category 39).

Canada:

Exactly 50 per cent foreign-owned establishments are included in the "+ 50 per cent" category.

United States:

Data includes enterprises with revenues or assets equal to or more than $100,000.

Data given for enterprises which are 10-100 per cent foreign-owned.

Category 35 includes all petroleum-related activities (exploration, production, refining and distribution).

Tobacco, leather and non-metallic mineral products (except petroleum and coal) industries are included in ISIC 39 (other manufacturing industries).

Australia:

The industrial classification in the table is the Australian Standard Industrial Classification (ASIC).

Foreign control: an establishment has been classified as being under foreign control if a single foreign resident investor or foreign-controlled enterprise held at least 25 per cent of the paid-up value of voting shares in the enterprise operating that establishment, provided that there was no larger holding by an Australian-controlled enterprise or Australian resident individual. All establishments not classified under foreign control have been classified under domestic control (no foreign ownership).

Japan:

An enterprise where the foreign owners do not have the intention of participating in the management is not considered to be foreign-owned even if more than 20 per cent of the capital is in foreign hands.

Printing and publishing, rubber and petroleum and coal products are included in the other category (ISIC 39).

Netherlands:

Establishments of enterprises with 80 per cent or more foreign participation.

Austria:

The data does not include tanning and leather finishing nor printing.

Sweden:

Exactly 50 per cent foreign-owned enterprises are included in the 20 to 50 per cent category.

Portugal:

Exactly 50 per cent foreign-owned enterprises have been included in the "+ 50 per cent" category.

Plastic products are included in category 39.

Category 6 excludes restaurants and hotels.

Norway:

Data only include establishments with at least five persons employed (in some cases three persons).

Exactly 50 per cent foreign-owned establishments are included in the "+ 50 per cent" category.

[*] As given in OECD: _Penetration of multinational enterprises_, op. cit.

sales in chemicals, petroleum products, automotive products and electrical engineering. In food, tobacco and beverages, MNEs accounted for only 25 per cent of total sales and in metals only 15.2 per cent.

Similarly, the United Kingdom component study[4] which provides data on employment by industry, for both home and foreign MNE operations as well as for domestically-operating enterprises (see Annex tables I and II) confirms MNE concentration in certain sectors. Thus, over 80 per cent of employment in electrical engineering and in the broad category of petroleum and coal, plus chemical and allied industries, was accounted for by UK and foreign MNEs combined in 1975. In contrast, MNE operations were almost non-existent in timber and furniture and accounted for one-fifth or less of employment in metal manufacturing, metal goods and leather clothing and footwear; what employment there was in MNEs in the last two of these sectors in either 1975 or 1971 was almost entirely in UK-based MNEs. Nevertheless, both in the industries of high MNE concentration and in those of smaller MNE presence, the relative importance of multinationals increased from 1971 to 1975.

Replies received from governments in response to the survey conducted for the project among main industrialised market economy countries, provide further details of the distribution of MNEs in different industries[5] which are summarised below:

AUSTRALIA

In 1972-73, foreign MNEs in the Australian manufacturing industry were concentrated as follows: chemical, petroleum and coal products 74.7 per cent (of value added), transport equipment 54.6 per cent, other machinery and equipment 42.1 per cent, basic metal products 38.0 per cent, textiles 33.3 per cent, and food, beverages and tobacco 33.2 per cent.[6]

Foreign multinationals employed 66 per cent of those working in the chemical, petroleum and coal products industry.

In the transport equipment industry, foreign-controlled firms accounted for nearly half of the employment. Employment per establishment was ten times as large here for the average foreign-controlled establishment as for the average Australian establishment, and over twice as large in the "large enterprise" group (i.e. the 200 largest enterprises in 1972-73); by 1975-76 the average foreign MNE was almost three times as large as the average Australian establishment in the latter group.

In the machinery and equipment industry, the foreign MNEs' share of employment was 40 per cent and the average foreign establishment was almost seven times larger than the average Australian-controlled establishment (in 1972-73). Although in 1972-73 the "large enterprise" group establishments, whether multinational or not, were similar in size, by 1975-76 the average foreign establishment was considerably larger than the average Australian enterprise. On the other hand, while foreign-controlled establishments in the basic metal products industry were, generally, more than twice as large as Australian-controlled establishments, the reverse was true for the "large enterprise" group where the Australian-controlled establishments were twice as large in employment terms.

Table II.3: Number of persons employed in enterprises or establishments of
enterprises with foreign participation: countries by order of
rank in the manufacturing industry

International Standard Industrial Classification (ISIC)	Germany[2] (Fed. Rep.)	France[2]	U.K.[1]	Canada[1]	U.S.[2]
	1972	1975	1973	1974	1974
	a + b	a + b	a	a	a + b
Major Division 2. Mining and quarrying	34.7	...	...	49	23
Major Division 3. Manufacturing	1 854.2	842.1	821.5	770	644
31. Manufacture of food, beverages and tobacco	139.1	...	65.6	98	75
32. Textile, wearing apparel and leather industries	...	52.5	26.5	59	37
33. Manufacture of wood and wood products, including furniture	...	15.1	2.5	32	7
34. Manufacture of paper and paper products, printing and publishing	...	31.4	19.6	68	40
35. Manufacture of chemicals and chemical, petroleum, coal, rubber and plastic products	258.7	190.6	92.7	112	244
36. Manufacture of non-metallic mineral products, except products of petroleum and coal	...	36.3	13.2	23	...
37. Basic metal industries	235.3	67.7	21.0	25	60
38. Manufacture of fabricated metal products, machinery and equipment	977.8	406.6	526.3	320	128
39. Other manufacturing industries	...	10.6	54.0	29	75
Major Division 6. Wholesale and retail trade, restaurants and hotels	208.1	...	...	...	256

Source: Adapted from OECD: Penetration of multinational enterprises in manufacturing
industry in member countries, statistics updated at the end of 1978
(Paris, 1978).

a = Foreign participation exceeding 50 per cent.

b = Foreign participation between 20 and 50 per cent.

Australia[1]		Japan[2]	Netherlands[1]	Austria[1]	Sweden[2]		Portugal[2]		Norway[1]		Finland[1]	
1972/3		1975	1977	1973	1975		1975		1976		1976	
a	b	a + b	a	a	a	b	a	b	a	b	a	b
20.2	4.0	0.0	...	...	0.3	...	2.8	1.0)			0.0	...
306.2	63.8	200.0	177.7	148.8	53.3	25.9	44.5	33.6)	27.3	19.7	16.4	5.3
58.0		6.2	...	12.5	7.5	2.9	3.1	2.8	1.5	0.0	1.1	1.4
27.4		1.2	...	24.4	2.1	0.6	5.6	3.3	...	...	4.6	0.2
5.3		0.0	...	3.2	0.3	0.2	0.9	0.9	0.4	...	0.1	0.0
15.8		1.8	10.5	9.2	2.8	2.8	1.8	0.1	1.1	0.4	0.4	0.0
61.4		30.3	...	23.6	9.0	3.5	7.1	4.3	3.2	6.7	2.5	0.3
7.7		8.8	10.0	10.3	1.4	1.2	0.6	3.3	0.5	0.4	0.2	0.1
24.9		0.5	...	4.2	2.6	5.3	0.7	0.7	5.5	7.0	0.2	0.7
167.5		2.0	...	60.7	27.0	9.3	22.5	17.0	14.0	4.1	6.8	2.6
2.1		149.2	...	0.7	0.6	0.1	2.3	1.1	...	...	0.5	...
...		26.5	...	25.3	36.2	4.4	13.5	5.6	...	...	...	...

[1] Data based on establishments of enterprises.

[2] Enterprises data.

... = not available.

Table II.4: Importance of MNEs (foreign and German) for selected sectors of the manufacturing industry in the Federal Republic of Germany (1973)

MNE SHARE OF ENTIRE SECTOR (AS PERCENTAGE OF SALES)

51.3% / 6.8%	Chemical industry: 58.1% of DM 73,300 m.
64.5%	Petroleum mfg.: 64.5% of DM 41,400 m.
15.2%	Ferrous and non-ferrous metals: 15.2% of DM 76,100 m.
28.5% / 9.2%	Steel, mechanical eng. and vehicles: 37.7% of DM 162,700 m.
49.0% / 22.1%	of which: automotive ind. 71.2% of DM 56,900 m.
38.8% / 17.4%	Electrical engin.: 56.3% of DM 79,800 m.
9.6% / 15.3%	Food, beverages and tobacco: 25% of DM 92,600 m.
19.3% / 10.8%	Manufacturing industry as a whole: 30.1% of DM 723,700 m.

German MNE   Foreign MNE   Other firms

Source: Jungnickel et al: Einfluss multinationaler Unternehmen auf Aussenwirtschaft und Branchen-struktur der Bundesrepublik Deutschland (Hamburg, HWWA 1977), pp. 283-284 as reproduced in P. Bailey, op. cit. component study on the Federal Republic of Germany for this report, p. 34.

In the food, beverages and tobacco industries the average foreign-controlled establishment was over four times larger than the average Australian-controlled establishment in 1972-73. By 1975-76 the average size of the large foreign-controlled establishments had risen, while the size of the average large Australian establishment had fallen.

As in the United Kingdom, a tendency for MNEs to increase their share in employment in many industries has been noticeable in recent years.

AUSTRIA

According to a survey for 1973 the employment share of foreign enterprises by economic sectors was as follows: construction 3.8 per cent; mining, etc. 4.4 per cent; trade 8.8 per cent; and service industries 10.2 per cent (of which hotels and restaurants alone 0.9 per cent). The highest employment share of foreign enterprises was in manufacturing (20.1 per cent). As regards individual manufacturing industries, the share of foreign enterprises was as follows: plastics and rubber products 39.7 per cent; electrotechnical industry 37.0 per cent; pulp and paper 32.3 per cent; chemical industry 31.0 per cent; and mechanical engineering 29.1 per cent.

Data available for the end of 1975 (corresponding to a slightly different classification) indicate that foreign enterprises had, by then, the following (increased) employment shares: electronics 50 per cent; petroleum and chemicals 49.3 per cent; paper and wood products 34.6 per cent; and textiles and clothing 30.9 per cent.

CANADA

The relevant Canadian data are summarised in tables II.5 and II.6. It can be seen from table II.5 that, in 1974, nearly 30 per cent of all employees in the logging industry, almost half of the mining employees (except those employed in crude petroleum and natural gas industry and in services incidental to mining), and more than 40 per cent of those in the manufacturing industries, were in foreign-controlled MNEs. Further available breakdowns, not included in tables II.5 and II.6, indicate the following ratios for branches of mining: metal mines 45.7 per cent; coal mines 34.5 per cent; non-metal mines (except coal mines) 78.4 per cent; and quarries and sand pits industry 30.2 per cent. A further statistical refinement shows that 79.8 per cent of the iron, 54.3 per cent of the copper, gold and silver, all the asbestos and 62.6 per cent of the potash mining industry employees were in foreign-controlled establishments.

As regards the manufacturing industries (see table II.5) almost all of the tobacco products, more than 60 per cent of the rubber, plastics, machinery and electrical products employees; over 70 per cent of the employees in transportation equipment, chemicals and chemical products; and more than 90 per cent of petroleum and coal products employees were to be found in foreign-controlled establishments. Further statistical refinement shows a greater degree of foreign control in several branches of these industries (for instance, 86 per cent of employees in the motor vehicle parts industry).

Foreign MNE activities are unevenly distributed over the
Canadian provinces. In Ontario, which is a preferred location of
foreign MNEs, 52.9 per cent of employees in the manufacturing
industries were in foreign-controlled establishments. On the other
hand, Saskatchewan seemed to have the lowest percentage of foreign-
controlled enterprises (20.2 per cent of employees). In Ontario,
68.6 per cent of the machinery, 84.2 per cent of the transportation
equipment, 68.7 per cent of the electrical products, 97.4 per cent
of the petroleum and coal products and 77.1 per cent of the
chemical and chemical products industries' employees were in
foreign-controlled establishments (all data relate to 1974).[7]

Table II.5: Employment in foreign-controlled establishments
in Canada in the logging, mining and manufacturing
industries (1974)

		No. of establishments	No. of employees	Percentage of employees
LOGGING				
Foreign		112	17 074	28.7
Canada		3 141	42 417	71.3
	Total	3 253	59 491	100.0
MINING[1]				
Foreign		169	49 435	49.2
Canada		385	51 140	50.8
	Total	554	100 575	100.0
MANUFACTURING				
Foreign		3 955	769 946	43.0
Canada		27 580	1 016 031	56.9
	Total	31 535	1 785 977	100.0

Source: Statistics Canada: Domestic and foreign control
of manufacturing, mining and logging establishments
in Canada (Ottawa, 1974), table 2, pp. 6-11.

[1] Excludes crude petroleum and natural gas industry and
services incidental to mining.

Reproduced by permission of the Minister of Supply and Services
Canada.

Table II.6:   Manufacturing industries in which foreign-
              controlled establishments employ more than
              half the total employees in Canada (1974)

Industry	No. of employees	Percentage of employees
TOBACCO PRODUCTS		
Foreign-controlled enterprises	9 489	98.8
Canada-controlled enterprises	107	1.1
Total	9 596	100.0
RUBBER AND PLASTICS		
Foreign	34 128	62.9
Canada	20 045	37.0
Total	54 173	100.0
MACHINERY		
Foreign	55 730	62.4
Canada	33 425	37.4
Total	89 155	100.0
TRANSPORTATION EQUIPMENT		
Foreign	124 779	72.5
Canada	47 191	27.4
Total	171 970	100.0
ELECTRICAL PRODUCTS		
Foreign	86 419	64.8
Canada	46 785	35.1
Total	133 204	100.0
PETROLEUM AND COAL PRODUCTS		
Foreign	16 324	93.5
Canada	1 111	6.3
Total	17 435	100.0
CHEMICAL AND CHEMICAL PRODUCTS		
Foreign	61 703	77.2
Canada	18 092	22.6
Total	79 795	100.0

Source: Statistics Canada: Domestic and foreign control
          of manufacturing, mining and logging establishments
          in Canada, op. cit.

Reproduced by permission of the Minister of Supply and Services
Canada.

FINLAND

Foreign enterprises have concentrated their operations in Finland in three manufacturing branches: metal trades, chemicals and textile and clothing. In the service sector, such enterprises are mainly to be found in wholesale trade and agency business.

Of the workers employed by foreign enterprises, 55 per cent were employed in manufacturing enterprises, 37 per cent by trade firms and 8 per cent by firms engaged in other activities (1974).

FRANCE

Half of the employment provided by foreign enterprises in France is concentrated in three manufacturing industries: electrical engineering, chemicals and the automotive industry. As a general rule, it can be said that the proportion of foreign-controlled enterprises tends to increase with the size of the enter-prises (in production and employment terms). Whereas foreign-controlled firms account, employment-wise, for only 1.7 per cent of enterprises with 20-50 employees, their share rises to 26.6 per cent for enterprises with between 1,000-2,000 employees (in 1973). American-controlled enterprises accounted for a good 40 per cent of the labour force in all foreign-controlled firms operating in France, followed closely by enterprises from other EEC countries, which attained nearly the same percentage. As regards non-EEC European countries, Swiss enterprises had an important employment share (holding a slight edge over German and British enterprises).

In terms of regional distribution, the Paris region had the highest concentration of foreign enterprises (26 per cent of total manufacturing/employment in the region being provided by such firms, as against a country average of 18 per cent). An above-average share in manufacturing employment was noted in 1973 in Picardie, Haute-Normandie and Central France (about 20 per cent). An above-average ratio was found in the Alsace, Lorraine and Champagne regions. In another industrially, comparatively less-developed region, Brittany, the employment share of foreign MNEs was also significant. American MNEs' investment and employment share was higher in the Paris region, while German and Belgian enterprises tended to concentrate their activities in areas just across their borders.[8]

ITALY

Foreign investment in Italy by mid-1970 was found mainly in the following industries: petroleum (29 per cent); mechanical engineering (20 per cent); chemicals (17 per cent); and steel (13 per cent).

JAPAN

In 1977, approximately 200,000 workers were employed in foreign subsidiaries in the manufacturing industry in Japan. They were concentrated in the following industries: general machinery (41,833), electrical machinery (36,623), chemicals (30,307) and transport equipment (19,731), followed by petroleum and coal and the rubber products industries (each with over 14,000 employees). Of the 610 foreign firms in the manufacturing sector as a whole,

401 were of American origin, and they alone employed almost
140,000 persons. (Similarly, the employees of Japanese enterprises
abroad were concentrated in the manufacturing industry (i.e. 556,000
out of 643,000), the majority of them being in the textiles
(213,000) and electrical machinery (129,000) industries.)

NORWAY

The bulk of foreign-owned interests in Norway are to be found
within the electro-chemical, electro-metallurgical and electrotechnical industries. The proportion of foreign interests in other
branches of industry is not particularly high. No quantitative
are, however, on hand for these industries.

NEW ZEALAND

The available data suggest that there is some concentration of
subsidiaries of foreign enterprises in four manufacturing industries
(food, beverages and tobacco; textiles; wood, paper and chemical
products; and metals) and in mining and quarrying. The technological and market conditions in these industries offer scope to
large enterprise groups with access to capital and technical
expertise, i.e., primarily foreign MNEs.

SWEDEN

In 1976, 53,000 workers, or approximately half of the roughly
100,000 employees in foreign majority-owned enterprises in Sweden,
were found in manufacturing. Additionally, 36,000 were in trading
firms and 10,000 in other activities, mainly service industries.

Percentage-wise, the employment share of foreign enterprises
in the manufacturing sector is relatively small. It amounted in
1975 to 5.7 per cent (4.5 per cent in 1970). The employment share
of foreign enterprises in the various individual manufacturing
industries shows considerable variations from this average. Table
II.7 gives the breakdown for two manufacturing industries and for
wholesale trade in which the share of foreign-owned MNEs in employment was particularly marked.

Table II.7:   Percentage employment share of foreign MNEs in Sweden

	Per cent	
	1970	1975
Wholesale trade	15.9	20.9
Manufacture of chemicals, including rubber and plastic products	15.0	14.5
Manufacture of food, beverages and tobacco	5.5	10.1

Source: Swedish Government memorandum, op. cit.

The striking increase in the foreign MNEs share in the food,
beverages and tobacco industry from 1970-75 is explained largely by
the acquisition of Swedish enterprises by foreign MNEs.

MNE employment trends by
sector

Comparisons of the sectoral distribution of MNE activity with
the over-all sectoral trends in five leading industrialised
countries, shown in table II.1, suggest that MNEs tend to be most
active in the relatively few sectors in which manufacturing employment has either grown, or declined the least, during 1970-76. Several
of the industries which registered the greatest decline in employment, such as clothing and steel, and thereby causing great concern
to unions[9], are industries in which domestic enterprises rather than
MNEs, predominate.[10] Shipbuilding is another sector which is
currently facing great structural problems in Western Europe,
accompanied by a fall in employment; but it is also a sector in
which there is little American or West European foreign investment
and few MNEs (some Japanese enterprises however do have investment
shares in shipbuilding). This is not to say, of course, that MNE
activity does not exist at all in the sectors of major employment
decline in the industrialised world; but the data do suggest that
the bulk of MNE activity has tended to be, in recent years at least,
in sectors of relative (even if, during the 1970s, modest) employment growth or stability.

The association of multinational enterprises with sectors of
relative production and employment growth finds further confirma-
tion in some of the component studies contributed to the present
research project. Some of these studies also draw comparisons
between multinational and non-multinational enterprises in the
sectors involved. For example, research data, reviewed in the
Federal Republic of Germany component study[11], show that industries
with a significant number of MNEs such as chemicals, mechanical
engineering and automotive products, added some 493,000 new jobs
between 1962 and 1972; and that sectors with relatively low MNE
penetration, such as mining, iron and textiles, registered a
decline in employment totalling 438,000 jobs over the same period.[12]
Domestic MNEs played a particularly important role in some of
the sectors. For example, while employment in the chemical
industry as a whole rose by 6.6 per cent between 1966 and 1973,
employment in MNEs in the industry rose by 33.2 per cent (85,200
persons) and this was accounted for exclusively by MNEs based in
the Federal Republic of Germany. As a matter of fact, the employment in foreign MNEs, as well as in the domestic multinational
firms of the sector, actually decreased by 14.4 and 9.2 per cent
respectively.[13]

The strong association of MNEs (foreign-owned subsidiaries) with
specific growth sectors is also brought out by the Belgian component
study. The relevant data, presented in table II.8, show the net
employment change in foreign MNE subsidiaries in Belgium between
1968 and 1975. Major employment increases for this group of enterprises occurred in technology-intensive manufacturing industries,
such as electrical equipment, transport equipment and chemicals;
moderate increases occurred in machines and food, drink and
tobacco (a marketing-intensive industry); and decreases occurred
in textiles. Minimal changes were noted in other industrial sectors,
such as iron, steel and non-ferrous metals.

The association between MNEs and sectors of relative employment
growth or stability may or may not imply that MNEs played a causal
role in this relative growth or stability. While detailed
statistical breakdowns, such as those emerging from the data
found in the case studies for the Federal Republic of Germany

Table II.8: Employment increases (or decreases) in foreign multinational subsidiaries in Belgium, operational in 1968 and still active in 1975, by sector of activity.

	NEW ESTABLISHMENTS (A)			ACQUISITIONS (B)			TOTAL (A + B)		
SECTOR[2]	1968-75[1]	Vertical per cent	Horizontal per cent	1968-75[1]	Vertical per cent	Horizontal per cent	1968-75[1]	Vertical per cent	Horizontal per cent
1. Food, drink and tobacco	1 638	3.5	29.1	3 992	28.6	70.9	5 630	9.3	100.0
2. Textiles, clothing and footwear	- 166	- 0.4	- 42.3	- 226	- 1.6	- 57.7	- 392	- 0.6	100.0
2.1 Textiles	- 780	- 1.7	- 75.7	- 250	- 1.3	- 24.3	- 1 030	- 1.7	100.0
2.2 Clothing and footwear	614	1.3	96.2	24	0.2	3.8	638	1.1	100.0
3. Wood, paper and leather	785	1.7	90.8	80	0.6	9.2	865	1.4	100.0
4. Chemicals	9 311	19.9	83.2	1 874	13.5	16.8	11 185	18.4	100.0
5. Petroleum, rubber	1 016	2.2	62.9	599	4.3	37.1	1 615	2.7	100.0
6. Non-metallic minerals	1 121	2.4	119.3	- 181	- 1.3	- 19.3	940	1.5	100.0
7. Metals and machinery	33 113	70.8	81.0	7 780	55.9	19.0	40 893	67.3	100.0
7.1 Iron, steel and non-ferrous metals	227	0.5	71.4	91	0.7	28.6	318	0.5	100.0
7.2 Metal manufacturing	1 160	3.5	108.1	- 124	- 0.9	- 8.1	1 536	2.5	100.0
7.3 Machines	4 472	9.6	71.6	1 771	12.7	28.4	6 243	10.3	100.0
7.4 Transport equipment	13 156	28.1	89.7	1 505	10.8	10.3	14 661	24.2	100.0
7.5 Electrical engineering	13 564	29.0	74.9	4 537	32.6	25.1	18 101	29.8	100.0
TOTAL (1 to 7)	46 818	100.0		13 918	100.0		60 736	100.0	

Source: Adapted from Van Den Bulcke and Halsberghe: Belgian component study for the present project, op. cit., table 3.1, p.67.

[1] Absolute employment change between 1968 and 1975.

[2] Miscellaneous and non-classified are not included.

and Belgium provide some indicators in this matter (i.e. in the first case locally-based MNEs and in the second case foreign-based MNEs were engines of growth for certain industries and years), it could be in other instances that MNEs simply chose to invest in sectors which were growing for other reasons; if such were the case, the MNEs would be reflecting rather than determining the existing trends. It would appear, for instance, that in the United Kingdom, there was in some industries a general decline in employment by and large both in MNEs as well as in other enterprises (see table II.1). Also, in spite of a modest increase, in the early 1970s, in the numbers of persons employed by both foreign direct investors in the United Kingdom and in UK-owned MNEs (see tables I.5, I.9 and Annex tables to this chapter), total manufacturing employment in the United Kingdom dropped more rapidly than in other industrialised countries; it dropped not only in the declining industries of steel and wearing apparel, but also in industries associated elsewhere with growth or considerable MNE activity, or both. However, the author of the component study concludes, in an over-all assessment, that MNEs have performed and resisted employment declines better than other enterprises.[14]

Concentration of MNEs by size of enterprises

A 1979 OECD report[15] showed that, in relative terms, most enterprises (or establishments[16]) under foreign control were found:

- in the "1,000 or more employees" category in Australia[17];

- in the "1,000-1,999 employees" category in Canada;

- in the "500-1,999" category in France;

- in the 500-999" category in Sweden; and

- in the "100 million A.Sch. and more" category in Austria.

Thus, although there is some general evidence that MNE presence increases with firm size, there are proportionally less enterprises under foreign control in the highest size category in Canada and France than in the next highest category; in Sweden their number is even lower than the average in this latter category.

In the OECD study referred to, data by sector are only available for Canada, France and Sweden. They show, in particular, that in Canada enterprises under foreign control may be strongly represented even in the relatively low size groups (e.g. 100-199 employees); that seems particularly true of the mechanical engineering, transport equipment, electrical engineering and chemical industries. In the largest size categories, foreign penetration is particularly marked in the oil, plastics and rubber industries (all enterprises in these sectors employing more than 1,000 persons are under foreign control) and in the transport equipment industry.

In the case of France, the penetration rates vary very considerably from one size category to another, depending on the industry. Two extreme examples are: the pharmaceutical industry where foreign enterprises are strongly represented in all size categories (except the "2,000+" group); and the footwear industry (where only the "1,000+" size group shows a high rate of foreign penetration). In Sweden where, in general, enterprises under

foreign control are mainly to be found in the middle size group
(100-999 employees), foreign penetration is most marked in the[18]
"100-199 employees" size category of the non-metallic minerals
industry; in the "200-499 employees" category of food, wood and
wood products, in chemicals and basic metal industries and in the
"500-999 employees" category in textiles, paper and engineering.

Regional distribution of MNEs within countries

Several studies have concluded for some countries that the
growth industries in which MNEs dominate are usually implanted in
areas of heavy economic concentration.[19] However, there is also
evidence of an above-average employment contribution of MNEs in
less prosperous regions of various countries, such as the United
Kingdom (Scotland), Belgium, France, the Federal Republic of
Germany, Italy and Ireland, to mention a few of them.[20] It has
indeed been argued that during the decades of considerable
economic growth (1950s and 1960s) governments, especially in
Europe, did not need to look in their industrial policies at
foreign MNEs as agents of general employment creation. They were
rather considered by governments and unions more as instruments of
industrial modernisation both for the economy in general and for
industrially backward areas.[21] Southern Italy, on the other hand,
seems to be an example of a less successful interaction between
government and multinational enterprises in regional policy.[22]
Investments by multinational and other enterprises in the
economically weaker regions of industrialised market economy
countries as well as public policies of employment promotion in
general also do not seem to have significantly affected inter-
regional or inter-country migrations.[23]

Notes

[1] Food, drink and tobacco is another sector of important MNE
activity, especially for enterprises based in the United States
and the United Kingdom. However, since sectoral employment change
data, to which MNE-concentration indicators could be compared, is
not available, this sector is not included in table II.1.

[2] Included in International Standard Industrial Classification
(ISIC) Division 38 (tables II.2 and II.3 in this chapter).

[3] Aggregated according to the two-digit ISIC.

[4] Stopford, op. cit. component study to the present project.

[5] Unless otherwise indicated the data presented were obtained
from these government memoranda.

[6] Special report prepared at the request of the Australian
Government by the transnational corporations research project at
Sydney University, as part of the Government memorandum sent to
the ILO (Chapter I, footnotes 7 and 17). See also the component
studies prepared for this report (listed in the Appendix) for
additional data relating to other countries.

[7] Enterprises/establishments are regarded as "foreign-controlled" if 50 per cent or more of the share capital is in foreign hands.

[8] Information contained in "Les participations étrangères dans l'industrie française au ler janvier 1973", in Statistiques et Etudes financières No. 321, sept. 1975, op. cit.

[9] Stressed, in particular, by the World Confederation of Labour in reply to the ILO information request mentioned in the Preface to this report.

[10] It is conceivable, however, that the share of multi-nationals in certain declining industries, such as clothing, could increase if all smaller multinational enterprises were included in the statistics. Most of the available statistics exclude, for practical reasons, such smaller enterprises.

[11] P. Bailey, op. cit.

[12] R. Sträglin, et al., Weiterentwicklung der Input-Output Rechnung also Instrument der Arbeitsmarktanalyse (Nürnberg, Bundesanstallt für Arbeit, 1976). More recent estimates in fact show that "between 1970 and 1978 the number of workers in the textile industry dropped from 496,592 to 319,697 and in clothing from 384,489 to 259,529, representing a total loss of 301,955 jobs" in W. Krüer-Buchholz: "Restrict and revive", ILO Information, Vol. 15, No. 4 (Geneva, Oct. 1979), p. 7.

[13] Jungnickel, et. al., p. 304 and pp. 384, 386, 389. These figures are unadjusted and include acquisitions, etc.

[14] Stopford, op. cit., p. 45.

[15] OECD: Penetration of multinational enterprises and industrialised concentration, Industry Committee, Paris, 26 March 1979, p. 15. In this report the OECD addressed mainly two questions: (1) the dominant position exerted on a sector by a limited number of enterprises (i.e. the concentration issue); and (2) the relative size of the different firms established in the sector.

[16] 'Enterprise' is the larger (economic) concept; 'establishment' is the smaller, technical and local, unit.

[17] The report prepared for the Australian Government (and mentioned in footnote 17 of Chapter I) gives considerable detail also on this subject (see page 33 of this chapter). The report in question also mentioned that the average foreign-controlled enterprise was five times larger than the average Australian enterprise.

[18] The industries referred to correspond to the following Divisions of the International Standard Industrial Classification (ISIC): non-metallic minerals (ISIC 36); food (31); wood and wood products (33); chemicals (35) and basic metal industries (37); textiles (32); the paper industry (34) and the engineering industries (38).

[19] Gerd Junne, et al: Die Regionalverteilung ausländischer Investionen in der Bundesrepublik Deutschland (Constance, August 1975; mimeographed), p. 176 and Michael Hodges: Multinational corporations and national governments: A case study of the United Kingdom's experience, 1964-1970 (Westmead (UK), Saxon House, 1974), p. 44.

[20] See, for instance, J. Van Ginderachter: "Les entreprises multinationales et la politique régionale de la CEE" in Revue des sciences économiques, No. 48, June 1973, pp. 59-76; ILO: Social and labour practices of some US-based multinationales in the metal trades (Geneva, 1977), pages 32-33; P.M. Kendall and D.J. Parker: Feasibility study on investment from other countries in the least prosperous regions of the community, Vol. I and Final report: Impact of investment from other countries in the least prosperous regions of the community, Vol. II (London, Metra Consultants for the Commission of the European Communities (DG Regional Policy), August 1975); further indications to this effect are given in some of the replies of governments to the ILO survey undertaken for this project (footnote 7, Chapter I).

[21] Hans Günter: "Trade unions and industrial policies in Western Europe", in Steven J. Warnecke and Ezra N. Suleiman: Industrial policies in Western Europe (New York, Washington, London, Praeger, 1975), p. 112.

[22] See for instance, J.J. Boddewyn, D.D. Grosser: "American direct investment in Italy: distribution, profitability and contributions", Review of economic conditions in Italy, Sept. 1972 pp. 362-378.

[23] See in this context Jean Mayer: "The regionalisation of employment policies in Western Europe", in International Labour Review, Vol. 118, No. 4, July-August 1979, pp. 415-426.

ANNEX Table I: __Employment, by industry and foreign penetration, 1971, 1973, 1975__[1]

Industry	1971		1973		1975	
	Total ('000)	Foreign share(%)	Total ('000)	Foreign share(%)	Total ('000)	Foreign share(%)
Food, drink, tobacco	793	7	792	8	774	10
Coal and petroleum	37	13	37	14	36	31
Chemicals and allied industries	412	19	289	22	402	22
Metal manufacturing	546	5	500	4	485	4
Mechanical engineering	1 006	12	911	14	927	16
Instrument engineering	174	21	149	27	158	26
Electrical engineering	758	16	734	20	745	20
Shipbuilding, marine engineering and vehicles	967	16	974	18	964	19
Metal goods n.e.s.	547	4	544	6	532	8
Textiles	613	3	584	3	533	4
Leather, clothing, footwear	455	1	484	2	471	2
Bricks, glass, cement, etc.	287	4	284	5	265	7
Timber, furniture, etc.	262	1	277	1	272	1
Paper, printing, publishing	592	2	576	3	564	8
Other	336	15	339	16	340	17
TOTAL	7 830	9	7 616	11	7 468	12
Total foreign employment ('000)	-	743	-	822	-	926

Source: Stopford, op. cit. UK component study for this project, p. 31.

1 Includes public sector

ANNEX Table II: Employment by manufacturing and category of firms, 1971 and 1975 ('000s)

Industry	1971					1975				
	UK	UK(M)[1]	F	MNEs share (per cent)	TOTAL	UK	UK(M)[1]	F	MNEs share (per cent)	TOTAL
Food, drink and tobacco	428	306	59	46	793	350	345	79	55	774
Petroleum and coal refining	95 }	270 }	5	79	37	74 }	259 }	11	83	36
Chemicals and allied industries			79	79	412			94		402
Metal manufacturing	490	30	26	10	546	429	34	22	12	485
Mechanical engineering	678 }	340 }	125	43	1 006	533 }	342 }	149	49	927
Instrument engineering			37		174			41		158
Electrical engineering	191	446	121	74	758	119	480	146	84	745
Shipbuilding, marine engineering and vehicles	613	197	157	37	967	595	189	180	38	964
Metal goods n.e.s.	473	39	35	14	547	452	38	42	15	532
Textiles	432	165	16	30	613	367	142	24	31	533
Leather, clothing and footwear	353	96	6	25	455	375	86	10	20	471
Bricks, glass, cement, etc.	191	83	13	35	287	168	77	20	37	265
Timber, furniture, etc.	251	9	2	4	262	260	9	3	4	272
Paper, printing and publishing	479	100	13	19	592	427	89	48	24	564
Other	211	76	49	37	336	215	67	58	36	340
Diverse firms	-	330	-			-	370	-		
TOTAL	4 643	2 445	742	41	7 830	4 015	2 527	926	46	7 468

Source: Stopford, op. cit., UK component study for this project, p. 40.

1 Figures exclude estimates of employment in brewing and bakery companies that are related to distribution.

UK   = UK domestic
UK(M) = UK multinational
F   = Foreign-controlled

CHAPTER III

MNEs AND THE STRUCTURE OF EMPLOYMENT

Skill, qualification and salary mix

It was noted in Chapter I that, in all industrialised market economy countries for which comparative data are available, the share of foreign MNE subsidiaries in total industrial value added and the total wages bill exceeds their share in industrial employment (see table I.3). Foreign MNEs are thus often seen as paying higher wages and salaries, and/or earning higher profits than the average national industrial firm. However, some of these comparisons suffer from problems of data comparability. In particular, such differentials tend to diminish when comparisons are made for enterprises in the same industry or branch of industry, as earlier studies have noted[1], and more specifically, as have some of the component studies for this project, such as the Belgian study.[2] However, there are instances where such differentials can also be observed in specific industries; but the picture is not always a completely uniform one as is shown, for instance, by data available for Australia.[3]

Generally speaking, however, much of the observed difference in value added and wages bills between foreign MNEs (and also home country MNEs) when compared with the industrial sector as a whole, seems attributable to the concentration of MNEs in particular industries with relatively greater capital and research intensity and consequently greater value added per capita (as shown in Chapter II). This particular industry distribution of MNEs implies that, as a rule, they tend to employ, both in absolute and relative terms, more technicians, engineers, scientists and skilled marketing and distribution personnel than the average industrial enterprise. Undoubtedly, certain MNE specific characteristics may also influence the skill-mix[4] but, normally, the industry characteristics appear to be more determinant.

Differences in structural features of MNEs and exclusively domestic firms have been examined mainly for home country operations. Thus, studies in the United States have shown that the US enterprises which are multinational in scope tend to spend, on average, a higher proportion of their revenues on research and development (R and D) than do non-multinational US enterprises.[5] Since R and D is a highly skilled labour-intensive activity, these firms, as a rule, also employ a more than proportionate number of scientists and engineers.[6]

Similar evidence obtained from a study of the 85 largest manufacturing enterprises with home countries in continental Europe[7] showed that the enterprises with manufacturing establishments in seven or more different countries allocated considerably higher sums to R and D as a percentage of sales revenue than did enterprises with few or no foreign manufacturing operations.[8]

MNEs generally tend to undertake a majority, and sometimes all, their R and D activities in their home country, although exceptions are frequently noted. Some European firms have major R and D laboratories outside their home countries in Europe or in the United States, and some American MNEs do considerable R and D in Europe; a few MNEs do some R and D in developing countries, particularly in large countries such as India. A tendency towards wider geographical distribution of R and D activities by MNEs has been found in various studies.[9] In the United Kingdom, for which systematic data exists on R and D expenses, the percentages of total R and D expenditure and R and D employment attributable to foreign majority-owned subsidiaries in 1975 (17 per cent of expenses and 16 per cent of total R and D employment) were higher than the share of such foreign subsidiaries in total employment (12 per cent).[10] It might not be surprising, therefore, that another study concluded that, in general, the skill-mix in foreign subsidiaries had not been negatively affected by the R and D location policies of MNEs as it was similar to that in comparable domestic UK firms.[11]

Whether the skill-mix and/or the wage levels in the foreign subsidiaries of MNEs is, on average, really higher or even as high as in national enterprises within the same industry and of the same size, is a matter of debate in some industrialised host countries. Thus the Government replies for the ILO survey from Canada and Austria[12] reflect a concern with the fact that foreign MNEs in some sectors have apparently been reluctant to decentralise R and D activities to the subsidiary level; and that, therefore, compared to national companies in the same sector, the MNEs may employ and train proportionally fewer skilled technicians and scientists.

The Canadian Government has investigated this matter in some depth through a survey of "R and D policies of large companies in Canada" carried out in 1977. Of the 88 replies received, 52 were from foreign-controlled and 36 from Canadian-controlled enterprises. It was found by the survey that 34 of the foreign subsidiaries conducted R and D, as against 15 of the Canadian-controlled firms. Thus, the proportion of foreign subsidiaries undertaking R and D (65 per cent) appeared somewhat higher than that of Canadian-controlled companies doing R and D (42 per cent). Included among the subsidiaries were three mining companies, all of which had semi-autonomous R and D operations (i.e. the company had a product or process which did not duplicate that of the parent, and conducted R and D to improve its product or process, or to develop new ones). The survey also included nine electrical/electronics companies, eight of which both imported technology and engaged in R and D in the subsidiaries located in Canada.

Further investigations in the province of Ontario showed that in the automobile parts industry the US automotive MNEs do most of their research and development in the United States. The Canadian-based subsidiaries generally considered it uneconomic to compete with, or attempt to duplicate, the research skills available at corporate level.

In the electronics industry the basic research is also usually centralised in the headquarters of the parent company, with the Canadian subsidiaries carrying out development work. When a subsidiary becomes an independent company, it often develops its own R and D capability with resultant effects on employment structure. In a specific case, the switch to development of new or improved products in Canada has led to a decrease in the use of imported components, with corresponding positive employment consequences. In the pulp and paper industry, however, it was found that R and D expenditures in the Canadian subsidiaries of US firms were only slightly lower than in the United States units but that there was a fall in such expenditure in both countries.[13]

In Belgium, available data suggests that on average both Belgian enterprises (multinational as well as purely domestic) and foreign MNEs employed the same number of university trained personnel. Variations in the percentage employed by foreign MNEs were explained by the fact that subsidiaries whose parent enterprise was located close to the Belgian border could often operate with fewer university trained personnel. The same was true for research frequency, with there being little or no difference between foreign MNEs and purely domestic enterprises. With regard to the development of new products, however, it was found that Belgian MNEs tended to devote more efforts towards this (especially concentrated in chemicals, transport equipment, electronics, and wood and paper) while foreign MNEs were relatively more engaged in research on the adapting of the existing products and processes of the parent to the specific market conditions of the host country and local regulations. While Belgian firms appear to be more research intensive (in terms of measuring R and D expenditures as a percentage of sales), foreign MNEs in fact employ a higher percentage of research personnel (as compared to total personnel) than do Belgian enterprises. This difference is explained in part by the fact that many researchers are engaged in other tasks in the smaller subsidiaries and in part by the fact that foreign MNEs are more concentrated in chemicals, electronics and mechanical engineering, requiring a larger number of scientific personnel.[14]

Detailed and conclusive statistics are not available for most countries on the question of skill-mix in MNEs and other enterprises. The Belgian, Canadian, United Kingdom and Australian evidence referred to suggests that differences exist but that the situation may vary according to sector, enterprise and local context.

Changes in skill-mix over time

The question whether multinational enterprise operations change the employment skill-mix over time has been the subject of debate especially in connection with the controversy which has arisen in a few MNE home countries over actual or alleged "job-export" by such firms in deciding to invest or to transfer certain production lines abroad.

The evidence summarised in Chapter I suggests that employment in home country MNEs has tended to increase during the 1960s and 1970s, although the increase was sometimes small in the last years (especially after domestic acquisitions had been subtracted), and was usually smaller than the employment increases in the foreign operations of MNEs. This global evidence does not confirm the hypothesis of large-scale employment transfers from home countries in the sense that, in general, the total volume of employment in the home country operations of MNEs did not decline (but rather increased or remained stable in most cases) during the 1960s and 1970s despite greater employment expansion in subsidiaries abroad.[15] As this does not exclude, however, the "export" of individual jobs or of certain categories of jobs through production transfers or expansion abroad, the question arises of the impact of foreign operations of MNEs on the skill-mix of their labour force in the home countries.[16]

The nature of this change in skill-mix has been described in
general terms for the United States as follows:

> To the extent that US investment abroad eliminates jobs
> on a gross basis or, in the case of defensive investment,
> that the employees who lost their jobs would have lost
> them anyway, the skill, industry, and location mix of
> those eliminated jobs will differ from the characteristics
> of the jobs created through export stimulus and managerial-
> staff accretions as a result of the foreign operations ...
> It becomes a problem of a structural mismatch between the
> jobs eliminated and the jobs created, even if the latter
> dominate. One of the obvious results is that the jobs
> that are eliminated will be almost exclusively production
> jobs and, if the MNC parent is unionized, predominantly
> union jobs. Other staff, and occasionally managerial,
> jobs may be eliminated, but this is less frequent and the
> reabsorption of such workers in similar jobs in the same
> firm is much more likely than in the case of production
> workers ... The skill mix of [the jobs created] obviously
> does not conform closely to the jobs eliminated through
> substitution of foreign production for exports. Thus
> one tendency, on a priori grounds, is for an expansion
> of foreign investment to relatively reduce the demand
> for production workers and to expand the number of
> clerical, professional, skilled, and managerial workers
> within the same industry ...[17]

This observation is also valid, with some adaptations, for other
industrialised home countries for MNEs.

While this tendency can be clearly seen from the empirical
analyses reviewed in the context of "employment export" in the next
chapter, it is, unfortunately, rather difficult to isolate
quantitatively from other change factors the structural change that
may be created in the labour market as a consequence of international MNE investment decisions. A 1973 study by Jose de la
Torre et al[18] made such an effort (using data from US Department of
Commerce case studies) by comparing the skill-mix of US industries
that made foreign investments with the average skill-mix of US
import-competing industries and with the industry averages. The
findings conform broadly with the a priori expectations outlined
above. The jobs created in the enterprises with foreign investment
activity were proportionately more numerous in the professional and
skilled categories and proportionately less numerous in the semi-
skilled, unskilled and clerical and sales categories than for
import-competing industries generally. Likewise, the jobs created
in the US as a result of foreign investment were more heavily weighted
towards professional workers than the industry average and less
heavily weighted towards semi-skilled and unskilled workers. The
findings regarding skilled jobs and clerical and sales jobs were
less clear-cut in the Jose de la Torre study.

Specific evidence of a relationship between multinational
operations and skill-mix changes over time also emerges from a
recent, well-documented case study in the Swedish welding-equipment
industry and, specifically, relating to two Swedish-based MNEs in
that industry prepared as a component study to the present research
project.[19]

In the context of a nearly 35 per cent drop in total domestic
Swedish employment in the welding-equipment industry between 1965
and 1977 (almost all of which had in fact occurred between 1965
and 1973), it was found:

- that there was a small increase in total home-country
  employment in the two sample MNEs in the industry, in
  contrast to the marked decline in domestic firms;

- that there was an especially rapid increase in staff
  employment (in the two sample MNEs), whereas production employees had dropped slightly, but less than
  for (non-MNE) national firms.

While the drop in numbers of production workers for the MNE
firms was somewhat smaller than that for national firms, the
composition of employment was rather different in the MNEs and
appeared to become more weighted towards staff and managerial
employment over time.   Whereas in non-MNEs in the welding equipment industry, production workers accounted for 75 per cent of
total employment in 1973 and 77 per cent in 1977, this proportion
was 51 per cent in 1965, 59 per cent in 1973 and 45 per cent in
1977 for one of the sample MNEs and 45 per cent in 1973 and 27 per
cent in 1977[20] for the second sample MNE.

Such structural change, whatever its origin, obviously creates
more labour market strains in a situation of reduced growth, than
in the earlier periods of unprecedented growth.   This lower growth
has been compounded by the arrival on the labour market of large
numbers of teenage job applicants.   During the 1950s and 1960s
governments usually promoted structural change in the interest of
over-all productivity increase;   and the unions, with few exceptions,
welcomed, or at least accepted it   as this since the majority of
the labour force visibly benefitted in terms of social upgrading
and increases in real wages.[21]   It may be recalled that, for
instance "... the governments of Japan, West Germany and
Switzerland, at times of overfull employment and inflationary
pressure, went to considerable lengths to urge their firms to drop
or to displace labor-intensive, low-productivity industrial
activities to other countries 'where the workers were'.   Micro-
economic 'job loss' has, at times, been seen as a positive good."[22]
However, "part of the current perception of 'job loss' is, of
course, due to the fact that many advanced country economies are
not now functioning at full-employment levels.   But if this macro-
economic malfunctioning is due largely to inadequate levels of
investment in physical and human capital, simply protecting
declining sectors is hardly likely to correct it."[23]

MNEs and the stability of employment

Despite particular MNE features, most of the government
replies received for the present study give the impression that as
regards employment security there is, on the whole, no significant
difference in industrialised countries between multinational and
other enterprises.   Still, as already indicated in an earlier ILO
study[24], it is sometimes feared that foreign enterprises, because
of their world-wide operations or management conception, are less
concerned with employment stability than the local firms. The main

question considered in this connection is whether multinationals react differently to changes in economic conditions than national enterprises. Some concern over such possible differences was expressed, for instance, in the reply by the Austrian Government to the ILO survey.[25] It was noted that foreign companies apparently tended to react more quickly to international economic and market changes than did local firms with labour force reduction plans (not necessarily decisions). Concern was also expressed regarding certain foreign investments made for short-term returns with possible negative effects on employment stability; and the possibility of negative employment repercussions of economically depressed parent companies on viable Austrian subsidiaries was likewise mentioned. In the over-all assessment, however, it was not inferred that employment security in Austria was different in foreign-controlled enterprises as compared to domestic ones. Likewise, the Austrian unions held that "job exports" and related employment security problems were on the whole not an important issue in the country given the relatively full employment position of Austria even at the present time.[26]

Couched in rather similar terms, the Canadian Government's response to the ILO survey refers to the possibility that, in a period of recession, the Canadian operations of foreign MNEs may be closed down or reduced before they are closed down or reduced in the home country of the MNEs. According to this reply such a possibility would, however, very largely depend on the type of enterprise operation and the market served by the Canadian subsidiary. Thus, recession in the home country would have little effect on the operations of a Canadian subsidiary established to serve the Canadian market. There was no indication in the government reply that such eventualities have indeed led to particular employment stability problems in Canada.

Employment stability in MNEs has come to be of particular importance in countries such as Belgium, and regions such as Scotland, which built up much of their pre-1974 industrial prosperity by receiving and encouraging inward investment and job creation by MNEs. Recently, there have been some highly publicised plant closures by MNEs in both Belgium and Scotland which have served to exacerbate oft-expressed union and government fears that employment in host-country MNE subsidiaries was inherently unstable. As in the Canadian case, the major cause for concern has been the possibility that in times of economic downturn, MNEs may give preference to home-country operations; and where changes in exchange rates have turned export-oriented foreign subsidiaries into high-cost plants, such fears have been further compounded. While detailed studies on these matters are not generally available, the data received seems to support the hypothesis that, whether as a result of MNE policy or of labour legislation applicable to all enterprises, the propensity of MNEs to close down enterprises or to undertake mass dismissals has usually been no greater than that of national firms.

Specific data on this question are provided in the Belgian component study. As far as the sectoral distribution of closures and employment losses is concerned, the Belgian component study notes that there was little difference between foreign and Belgian-owned companies. Almost half of the Belgian enterprises that closed down during the period reviewed did so as a result of bankruptcy, and 12 per cent were for other economic reasons. On the other hand, only one-quarter of the foreign subsidiaries went bankrupt while more than 40 per cent wound up their operations because of other economic considerations. The study concludes that the expansion of foreign enterprises could not be maintained during 1975-78, however. The crisis which started in 1974 resulted in the cancellation of many investment projects and in the shutdown of a number of existing plants and divisions as well as in collective dismissals. The net annual growth rate of employment for 1975-76 was thus only 0.4 per cent against 5.1 per cent for 1968-75. Yet there are indications that foreign subsidiaries were better able to resist the effects of the economic crisis than local firms as the Belgian industry as a whole experienced in 1975-77 alone a loss of 77,965 jobs (annual rate of -3.97 per cent). The fear of a massive withdrawal of foreign MNEs from Belgian territory has certainly not materialised. It would seem that the relatively favourable employment performance of foreign enterprises as compared with Belgian companies is connected with a relatively higher productivity and profitability of the foreign enterprises and the fact that their integration in a larger multinational group possibly gives them more leeway to absorb temporary difficulties.[27] Thus, somewhat in contrast to other evaluations, in the Belgian case the international character of MNEs has been regarded as a positive factor for employment stability.

Table III.1: Percentage changes in United Kingdom employment by industry and category of firm, 1971-1975

| Industry | Controlled by UK enterprises with | | Foreign-controlled MNEs | Total |
	domestic character	multinational character		
Food, drink, tobacco	- 18	+ 13	+ 34	- 3
Coal and petroleum	- 22	- 4	+ 25	- 2
Chemicals and allied inds.				
Metal manufacturing	- 12	+ 13	- 15	- 11
Mechanical engineering	- 21	+ 1	+ 11	- 8
Instrument engineering				
Electrical engineering	- 38	+ 8	+ 21	- 1
Shipbuilding, marine engineering and vehicles	- 3	- 4	+ 15	- 0
Metal goods n.e.s.	- 4	- 3	+ 20	- 3
Textiles	- 15	- 14	+ 50	- 13
Leather, clothing, footwear	+ 6	- 10	+ 67	+ 4
Bricks, glass, cement, etc.	- 12	- 7	+ 54	- 8
Timber, furniture, etc.	+ 4	0	+ 50	+ 4
Paper, printing, publishing	- 11	- 11	+369	- 5
Other	+ 2	- 12	+ 18	+ 1
Diverse firms		+ 21		
All manufacturing	- 14	+ 3	+ 25	- 5

Source: UK component study, J. Stopford, op.cit., p. 41.

Some specific data are also available for the United Kingdom and more particularly for Scotland, but only up to 1975. Thus, a full analysis of the reactions of MNEs to the turbulent conditions in the wake of the oil crisis is not yet possible.[28] The United Kingdom component study notes for the period up to 1975 that as a whole "...the overwhelming impression is that of stability rather than [negative] change"[29] even taking into account acquisitions for which no quantitative data are on hand, particularly for employment in foreign MNE subsidiaries. Thus Table III.1, drawn from the UK study, actually shows some employment increases in foreign-controlled subsidiaries from 1971 to 1975, while most employment declines were concentrated in UK domestic firms. With regard to Scotland, a recent relevant study shows that a very rapid build-up of US investments in Scotland during the late 1960s was followed, a decade later, by readjusted policies. Thus certain US firms have apparently used the Scottish site as a "...springboard for Europe... and now wish to adjust their production policies and production mix"[30] in line with changing conditions; Scotland seems especially vulnerable to such change at the present time.

Fears about employment security in MNEs have also been related to a recent "disinvestment" phenomenon[31], coming upon a period of unprecedented growth and MNE expansion in Europe. Indeed, according to a 1979 study, between 1967 and 1975, American MNEs withdrew 30 per cent of their investments from the original six Common Market countries through closures of production units or reduction in the degree of capital participation in their subsidiaries below 20 and 10 per cent; and MNEs from EEC member States reduced their investment by 26 per cent. Such American "disinvestment" occurred more rapidly between 1971 and 1973 than in the subsequent years, whereas "disinvestment" by EEC countries rose between 1972 and 1975.[32]

It has been noted, however, that the available evidence does not seem to reveal, on the whole, significant differences as regards "disinvestment" behaviour (especially if understood as a reduction in new investments) between exclusively domestically operating firms and MNEs, or between European and American multinationals.[33]

Notes

[1] Comparable data for MNEs and exclusively domestic enterprises of the same size and economic characteristics are not generally available. See in this context also, ILO: Wages and working conditions in multinational enterprises (Geneva, 1976).

[2] D. Van Den Bulcke and E. Halsburghe, component study for this project, op. cit.

[3] The Australian government reply to the ILO survey (see Chapter I, footnote 17) permitted comparisons within specific industries between value added and wages per employee for both Australian and foreign firms, as well as for larger ones of both types. In most industries, value added per employee tended to be higher for all foreign-controlled enterprises, including the larger ones, than for Australian enterprises. However, in some industries, such as food, beverages and tobacco, and paper and paper products,

the value added rose much faster for Australian-controlled enterprises between 1972-1976 thus reducing differentials between foreign and domestic enterprises. Similarly, in most industries wages tended to be higher in foreign-controlled enterprises, with the exception of food and beverages in 1975-76. Still, wages in the larger Australian firms in this sector were 14 per cent higher than in the larger foreign firms. In the clothing and footwear industry, where foreign MNEs had been leading employers in earlier years, the situation had been reversed by 1975-76 with the larger Australian firms paying slightly higher wages. By 1976, in the paper products sector, too, the larger Australian firms were showing higher wages and value added per employee. Although value added had been high for the larger Australian firms in 1972-73 in the fabricated metal products sector, the figures for foreign and domestic enterprises were rather similar by 1975-76. The wages paid in domestic enterprises were marginally higher in this sector than in the foreign enterprises; and the same was true for the transport equipment sector.

[4] This includes characteristics such as the domestic job repercussions of MNE expansion abroad, dealt with in the next section.

[5] James W. Vaupel, op. cit., p. 11.

[6] Raymond Vernon, Sovereignty at Bay, op. cit., Chapter I.

[7] Belgium, France, Federal Republic of Germany, Italy, Netherlands, Luxembourg, Sweden and Switzerland.

[8] Lawrence G. Franko, The European multinationals, op. cit., p.19.

[9] D. Creamer: Overseas research and development by United States' multinationals 1966-1975 (New York, The Conference Board, 1976). For a more recent study see R. Ronstadt: Research and development abroad by US multinationals (New York, Praeger, 1977) and "International R and D: The establishment and evaluation of R and D abroad by several U.S. multinationals" in Journal of International Business Studies (Spring 1978), Vol. 9, No. 1, pp. 7-24. A review of these and other literature on this subject is given in S. Lall: "The international allocation of research activity by US multinationals", in Oxford Bulletin of Economics and Statistics, Vol. 41, No. 4, November 1979, pp. 313-331.

[10] OECD: Penetration of multinational enterprises in manufacturing industry in member countries. Statistics updated at the end of 1978, op. cit., pp. 3 and 18.

[11] J. Gennard and M.D. Steuer: "The industrial relations of foreign-owned subsidiaries in the UK", in British Journal of Industrial Relations, 9(2), July 1971, pp. 143-159.

[12] The memorandum of the Austrian Government indicated that with regard to research and development, the contribution of MNEs was not as great as it could be since most research and development was done in the home country (see footnote 7, Chapter I).

[13] The Canadian experience was indicated in the Government memorandum for the ILO survey for this project and included findings of a Select Committee in the Province of Ontario.

[14] D. Van Den Bulcke: Belgian industrial policy and foreign multinational corporations: objectives versus performance. (Berlin, International Institute of Management, Science Centre, Oct. 28-29 1980; mimeographed paper presented at a conference on MNC-Government Relations: Policy Issues), pp. 25-30. For data on this subject in Sweden see Lars Hokonson: R and D in foreign-owned subsidiaries in Sweden (Berlin, International Institute of Management, Science Centre, Oct. 28-29 1980; mimeographed paper presented at a conference on MNC-Government Relations: Policy Issues).

[15] Whether or not these increases in MNE employment at home could have been larger in the absence of direct foreign investment of MNEs is an issue that has been subjected to specific research which is discussed in Chapter IV relating to the role of MNEs in the restructuring of industry.

[16] The question is also raised of the impact of such expansion abroad on the skill-mix in developing host countries for which little information is available.

[17] Hawkins and Jedel, op. cit., pp. 68-70.

[18] Jose de la Torre, Jr., Robert B. Stobaugh, and Piero Telesio: "US multinational enterprises and changes in the skill composition of US employment", in Duane Kujawa (ed): American labor and the multinational corporation (New York, 1973), pp. 127-143.

[19] Jordan and Vahlne, op. cit (see list in Appendix).

[20] Ibid., see their table 11, p. 18.

[21] Hans Günter: "Trade unions and industrial policies in Western Europe", in Warnecke and Suleiman (eds): Industrial policies in Western Europe, op. cit., pp. 93-117.

[22] Lawrence G. Franko: "Foreign direct investment in less-developed countries: Impact on home countries", in Journal of International Business Studies, Winter 1978, p. 59.

[23] Ibid.

[24] ILO: Wages and working conditions in multinational enterprises, op. cit., p. 46.

[25] Referred to in footnote 7, Chapter I.

[26] The reports in question referred rather to the issue of "job imports"; MNEs in the past were said to have tended to concentrate in the built-up areas where labour was scarce and to have provoked the inflow of larger numbers of foreign "guest" workers.

[27] Van Den Bulcke and E. Halsberghe, Belgian component study, op. cit., esp. pp. 27 and 51. See also D. Van Den Bulcke, J.J. Boddewyn, B. Martens and P. Klemmer, Investment and disinvestment policies of multinational corporations in Europe, op. cit.

[28] Stopford, UK component study, op. cit., p. 28.

[29] Ibid., p. 27.

[30] N. Hood and S. Young: European development strategies of US-owned manufacturing companies located in Scotland, Scottish Economic Planning Department (Edinburgh, HMSO, 1980).

[31] The term "disinvestment" is used in the literature with various connotations, such as closure of enterprises, decrease in new investments and alternative investment decision-making (e.g. preference for other countries as locations for MNEs).

[32] Van Den Bulcke et al: Investment and disinvestment policies of multinational corporations in Europe, op. cit., pp. 32-36.

[33] Ibid., pp. 55-57 and "Politiques d'investissement, réductions ou cessations d'activités de multinationales en Europe", in Multinational Info (Brussels), No. 1 (1979), p. 12. See also D. McAleese and M. Counahan: "'Stickers' or 'Snatchers'? Employment in multinational corporations during the recession", in Oxford Bulletin of Economics and Statistics, vol. 41, No. 4 (Nov. 1979), pp. 345-358.

CHAPTER IV

MNES AND THE INTERNATIONAL RESTRUCTURING OF
INDUSTRY, INCLUDING THE "JOB EXPORT" ISSUE

MNEs, independent agents for change?

The scope which MNEs may have for transferring activities
between countries has sharpened fears that such enterprises may
enjoy considerable discretionary power to act as independent agents
in promoting the international allocation of resources and employment. The relatively sudden emergence, during the past decade, of
a few so-called "newly-industrialising countries" (NICs) as
significant exporters of manufactured goods, partly as a result of
MNE activities, has further compounded this preoccupation,
especially among trade unions in industrialised countries.[1]

In fact, certain consumer goods industries in the
industrialised countries, including clothing, footwear, textiles
and electronics, have distinctly felt the impact of competition
from exports from the newly-industrialising countries. And it is
feared that these same NICs are having, or will have, a similar
impact on shipbuilding and steel, two other industries which
provide a large, but rapidly declining, number of jobs in the
industrialised nations.

While these job losses have a variety of origins, including
technological developments, general demand factors, international
competition between national enterprises, international subcontracting[2] and the like, losses of export opportunities through
"market-oriented" foreign MNE investments and import competition
generated by overseas "supply-oriented" MNE subsidiaries are likewise relevant. Multinational management tends to explain investments abroad as reflecting imperative requirements of markets and
competition, i.e. global change factors calling for such adjustment
by multinational enterprises in the interest of efficient production
and ultimate survival. Its critics see the search for profits as
the driving factor.

The available evidence is mixed as to the extent to which
multinational enterprises do, or can in fact exercise discretion in
decisions to transfer production abroad on a large scale,
especially to low-wage developing countries. Instances can be
found of multinational enterprises apparently having set up "off-
shore sourcing subsidiaries" in Hong Kong, Singapore or elsewhere,
before they were obliged to do so in self-defence, by competition
in home or export markets, either from local firms or from multinational enterprises based in other home countries.[3] On the other
hand, examples can be found where such foreign subsidiaries were
set up only after substantial competition, for instance from
national enterprises in NICs, had been encountered in home or third
markets.[4] Still other cases exist - notably in the US television
industry - where some MNEs resisted production transfers abroad
until they were thrust upon the firm by imminent bankruptcy.[5]

The problem for the researcher is that, in all such cases, observable events must be compared with hypothetical, non-observable alternatives. Thus, a clear-cut general answer as to the degree to which MNEs have been wilful, discretionary agents of production transfers abroad, is not possible. For this purpose, the actual decision-making processes of individual multinationals, although they would still include hypotheses regarding the parameters of possible alternative behaviour, would need to be investigated through detailed case studies.

Leaving aside the debate of the motives of MNEs in investment decisions, the question remains of the role of multinational enterprises in the cycle of transferring production processes towards developing countries.[6] The suspicion that MNEs play a particularly important role is strong among many unionists and a number of academics on both sides of the Atlantic. Within the United States the debate centres on the role played by tariff items 807.00 and 806.30 (which exempt American components from import duties if they re-enter the US as part of a product assembled abroad); within Europe, the debate has been less structured but is increasingly concentrated on the role of the MNEs in the "offshore assembly" phenomenon (which, in practice, is what the United States tariff items encourage). Provisions exist, for example, in the Federal Republic of Germany and the Netherlands for "offshore assembly"[7] and international subcontracting might become more important under the General System of Preferences of the United Nations Conference on Trade and Development (UNCTAD).[8]

Role of multinationals in the exports from developing countries

The available figures on the MNE role in developing countries' exports (see tables IV.1 and IV.2) seem to suggest that the multinationals indeed play a not negligible, but not the major role in transferring manufacturing production lines to developing countries and exporting from these; and thereby becoming suppliers of imports to industrialised countries. They also show that the involvement of MNEs varies greatly according to country and region.

Table IV.1 set out the approximate share of multinational manufacturing enterprises in the manufactured exports of selected developing countries. It is apparent that MNEs in Latin America play a much more important role in manufacturing for export than they do in Asia. On the whole, however, this role is relatively small in most developing regions. Thus, from 1966 to 1974, subsidiaries of US enterprises were, on the average, responsible for 23.1 per cent of manufactured exports in the case of Latin America, 5.5 per cent in Africa, 1.7 per cent in the Middle East, 6.1 per cent in the rest of Asia and 9.2 per cent for the developing countries as a group (weighted annual averages).[9]

This relatively small share of multinational enterprises in the export of manufactures from developing countries is hardly surprising. Undoubtedly, in the past two decades, the prime motive of direct foreign investment by multinationals in developing countries has been to enter the usually protected markets of these countries and not the winning of export platforms, as the following data tend to illustrate. During the period 1966-74, local sales by the majority-owned manufacturing subsidiaries of US enterprises in developing countries constituted 90.5 per cent of total sales. The proportion was as much as 94 per in Latin America and 86 per cent in the Middle East, while it was somewhat smaller, that is 75 per cent, in Asia and Africa. It is interesting to note that for the developing countries as a group, this proportion has changed very little over time, standing at 91.6 per cent in 1966, 91.0 per cent in 1970 and 89.4 per cent in 1974 for the before-mentioned regions, respectively. While recent years have witnessed a growth in manufacturing for exports by MNE subsidiaries located in developing countries, it is important to keep in mind the magnitudes referred to in considering the role of multinationals in the international restructuring of industry and trade. In this context it must be recalled also that the bulk of MNE investments still go to industrialised countries and that in 1975 $194,250 million was invested in these countries (i.e. 74 per cent of the total stock of foreign direct investment).[10]

What is becoming apparent in this analysis is that in addition to MNEs, many other agents of change, including changing general competitive patterns on world markets and industrial policies of developing countries, have been involved in the international restructuring of industry and trade which has resulted in exports of manufactured goods of developing countries rising from less than 4 per cent of OECD manufactured imports in 1968 to more than 8 per cent in 1977.[11] The influence of these other factors must have been more important than that of the MNEs alone.

Table IV.1: Share of MNE manufacturing enterprises in the exports of manufactures from selected developing countries

Country	Approximate share in per cent	Year of estimate	Total manufactured exports in 1972: US $ million
Argentina	At least 30	1969	394
Brazil	43	1969	749
Colombia	30 or more	1970	172
Hong Kong	10	1972	2 635
India	Approx. 5	1970	1 320
Korea (Rep. of)	At least 15	1971	1 351
Mexico	25-30	1970	647
Pakistan	5-10	1972	380
Singapore	Nearly 70	1970	893

Source: Deepak Nayyer: "Transnational corporations and manufactured exports from poor countries", in Economic Journal (Cambridge University Press), March 1978, vol. 88, p. 62.

Table IV.2: Number of manufacturing subsidiaries for the 186 largest US-based MNEs in clothing, steel and consumer electronics, with exports greater than 10 per cent of sales in 1975

Country or region	Textiles, clothing	Iron and steel	Radios, TVs and appliances
CANADA	3	1	2
LATIN AMERICA	1	0	7
of which			
MEXICO	1	0	4
BRAZIL	0	0	1
EUROPE	19	6	12
of which			
PORTUGAL, GREECE and TURKEY	0	0	0
SPAIN	0	0	1
N. AFRICA AND MIDDLE EAST	1	0	0
EAST AND WEST AFRICA	0	0	0
SOUTH ASIA	0	0	1
of which			
INDIA	0	0	0
EAST ASIA	1	0	7
of which			
HONG KONG	0	0	3
JAPAN	1	0	1
SINGAPORE	0	0	1
REPUBLIC OF KOREA	0	0	0
AUSTRALIA	1	0	2
TOTAL EXPORT SUBSIDIARIES	28	7	31
of which:			
EXPORT SUBSIDIARIES IN DEVELOPING COUNTRIES	2	0	12
TOTAL MANUFACTURING SUBSIDIARIES WORLD-WIDE	149	57	115

Source: Harvard Multinational Enterprise Project, as cited in Joan P. Curhan, William H. Davidson and Rajan Suri: Tracing the multinationals (Cambridge, Mass., Ballinger Publishing Company, 1977), pp. 400-403.

The role of MNEs in the international restructuring of industry and trade, in terms of its significance for industrialised countries, might thus be summarised as follows:

(1) MNEs, particularly US and Japanese MNEs, have concentrated their investments in manufacturing mostly in those newly-industrialising countries which have had the greatest export performance. Thus, some two-thirds of all US MNEs manufacturing investments in the developing world are concentrated in Mexico, Brazil, the Republic of Korea, Singapore, Hong Kong, Argentina, India and the Philippines. A similar, if not greater, proportion of total Japanese foreign manufacturing investments is concentrated in several of these countries, in addition to Indonesia, Thailand and Malaysia.[12] Majority-owned, foreign subsidiaries of US enterprises, located in developing countries, accounted for about 8 per cent of the manufactured goods exported by these countries in 1975 (which amounted to $33,200 million).[13] The proportion of US MNEs' exports as a percentage of all manufactured exports ranged from 5 per cent in Asia to 18 per cent in Latin America and the Caribbean (counting fully US-owned and majority US-owned subsidiaries). Inclusion of subsidiaries of non-US MNEs and minority joint ventures might approximately double the total figure for developing countries (it would probably not double the Latin American or Caribbean percentages, given the considerable preponderance of US foreign investment in these regions).[14]

(2) Considering that the US multinational enterprises account for somewhat under half of foreign manufacturing investments in less developed countries, approximately 20 per cent of the manufacturing exports from these countries (mainly from NICs) may be linked at present to MNE activity of all national origins.[15] A substantial fraction of these exports (about one-third) went to other developing countries in the 1970s.

(3) A new factor to be considered in the context is the growth of Free Trade or Export Processing Zones through which MNEs have been attracted and MNE exports from developing countries have increased. These now exist in some 30 countries and many other countries plan to establish such zones. Still, thus far the proportionate importance of these zones in total exports from developing countries is small.[16]

(4) In many of the newly-industrialising countries, Hong Kong being a particularly striking example, local entrepreneurs aided by trading houses and retailing chains, rather than manufacturing MNEs, have been a decisive factor in the development of exports.[17]

(5) Most MNE activity in the NICs has been oriented to producing for local markets as "import-substituting investment" rather than to producing for export (with the possible exception of some Japanese MNE investments which often seem more export-oriented).

(6) MNEs in the industrialised countries are largely concentrated in growth industries and are less noticeable in industries where the greatest structural problems - and employment adjustments - are presently encountered (e.g. textiles, clothing, footwear and steel - see Chapter II). The question must be asked,

however, whether the exports from foreign subsidiaries of MNEs in
these declining industries had a general and decisive influence on
the structural changes in the home countries. While this is a
rather difficult question to answer, there are indications that
this has not been so, at least in the case of the United States,
as evidenced by data pertaining to the degree to which US imports
in sectors of notable export performance of less developed
countries have been "related-party" transactions between subsidiaries and US parent companies (see table IV.3). On the whole,
and despite a handful of clear exceptions, MNE links in textiles,
clothing and footwear have not been numerous (see tables IV.2 and
IV.3). In steel, there appear to be few export-oriented MNE subsidiaries anywhere in the world - at least of United States' MNE
parentage. As far as these industries are concerned, it would
therefore be difficult to substantiate the argument that multinational enterprises have been the major agent in the transfer of
employment out of the industrialised countries involved. It must
be remembered in this connection that locally-owned, domestic firms
in several developing countries, such as Hong Kong, have been very
successful in exporting relatively standardised competitively-
priced goods; and subcontracting arrangements by non-MNEs as well
as MNEs are likewise important. Other institutional agents of
change include trading companies and retail and import houses.
MNEs, as such, appear to be one change agent but not the major
one, as compared to others, at least as far as the industries
referred to earlier are concerned.

(7) The MNEs role is certainly very different in trade
between developing and industrialised countries with respect to
certain technology-intensive and labour-intensive products, such
as electrical machinery, including radios, TVs and appliances,
and scientific instruments and machinery. "Related party" imports
into the United States as a percentage of total imports from
various NICs are very important in the electrical machinery
category, bordering on 100 per cent in the case of US imports from
Singapore, Malaysia, Mexico and Brazil (see table IV.3). East-
Asian export subsidiaries, notably absent in the portfolios of the
186 largest US MNEs in textiles, clothing and steel, are more
numerous in the case of radios, TVs and appliances (table IV.2).
However, these facts alone may or may not be indicative of a net
substitution of production and employment in product groups
comprising electrical machinery. Net increases in employment in
the industrialised countries taken as a group appear to have been
occurring, leaving room for the possibility that job losses in
certain countries may have been more associated with competition
from other advanced countries, rather than with MNE shifts of
production to developing countries whether as a result of changes
in trade patterns or of direct transfers of production lines. For
example, despite some use of "off-shore affiliates" or "border
plants" by US and European MNEs in consumer electronics, competition
(among industrialised market economy countries) from non-related
firms in Japan appears to have had a much more important impact on
this sector in the US and Europe than MNE activities in developing
countries.

Table IV.3: US related-party imports as a percentage of total imports of selected manufactured products, from selected "newly industrialising" developing countries, 1977

Country	Textiles 65*	Non-electric machinery 71*	Electric machinery 72*	Clothing 84*	Footwear 85*	Scientific instruments 86*	Total mfg.	Total mfg. import value ($ million)
Argentina	0.5	39.1	76.1	2.9	0.8	10.0	9.2	167
Brazil	9.2	59.9	95.3	18.0	0.5	38.4	38.4	755
Colombia	1.5	16.8	3.9	15.7	81.2	87.8	14.1	60
Mexico	9.6	87.8	95.6	68.0	60.9	93.6	71.0	1 798
Hong Kong	4.9	68.5	43.4	3.4	3.6	30.4	18.1	2 618
India	6.1	30.5	58.7	15.8	6.1	16.7	10.1	180
Korea (Rep.of)	5.5	64.2	67.3	7.1	1.8	12.1	19.7	2 328
Malaysia	0.2	83.2	97.0	1.9	0.0	91.9	87.9	385
Philippines	28.9	69.7	31.7	53.4	0.0	27.0	47.5	352
Singapore	4.3	90.5	97.0	0.5	0.0	85.3	83.3	630
Haiti	2.9	33.7	36.5	24.8	77.2	97.9	28.4	101

Source: G.K. Helleiner and R. Lavergne, "Intra-firm trade and industrial exports to the United States", in Oxford Bulletin of Statistics, vol. 41, No. 4 (Nov. 1979), p. 307.

* Standard International Trade Classification (SITC).

Adjustment to trade with developing countries

However, adjustment problems related to certain industrial imports from developing countries, whether they involve local enterprises or MNE subsidiaries in these countries) are sometimes important at the micro-economic (plant, enterprise, product line and sector) level. The sectors most highly penetrated by imports from developing countries - clothing, footwear, leather goods and certain categories of electrical products which require much hand assembly - are also among the most labour-intensive manufacturing sectors in the industrialised countries. Moreover, labour in these sectors is usually relatively unskilled and immobile, and therefore difficult to transfer to other occupations[18]; and the problems may be compounded where the workers directly affected are occupationally handicapped, e.g. by reason of age, sex, access to retraining, etc., or are unskilled new entrants into the labour force. In this connection it has been observed that job losses arising from competition from developing countries often require that the workers affected should upgrade their qualifications as otherwise they cannot be absorbed in their declining industries, or elsewhere, with their existing and usually low skills.[19] It is also clear that structural change or job losses, whatever their origin and magnitude, pose greater problems in periods of relative economic stagnation, such as the one prevailing over the past few years in many industrialised market economy countries, than in periods of unprecedented growth as was the case in the preceding decades. Thus, although the available global evidence does not permit one to ascribe to MNEs, world-wide, the main role in structural employment change and concomitant "job export", even relatively smaller production transfers in these enterprises (irrespective of the question of whether they are made necessary by competitive pressures or not) can, at the present juncture, arouse legitimate social concern on the part of labour and governments.[20]

Multinational enterprises and technology

A major source of rather widespread concern is the possible negative impact of new technologies, in particular the new micro-processor technology, on employment. As MNEs play a leading role in the development and utilisation of technology[21], they are largely associated with these problems. Since the debate on this matter goes beyond the framework of the present report, it suffices to point out that modern technological developments do not imply a unilateral reduction of employment or an acceleration of production transfers from the industrialised to the developing countries. In this context reference may be made to a recent study which concludes that the utilisation of micro-processors could slow down, and possibly reverse, certain processes of international production transfers. It is argued, in particular, that with the new technologies, and the relative reduction of unit/labour cost which they make possible, many labour-intensive industries may again become economically viable in the industrialised countries. The sectors which are already being affected by the micro-processor are, in part, the very sectors in which certain developing countries have been most successful in penetrating world markets - textiles, footwear, garments, electronics. According to the study, other activities, which thus far were also potential candidates for transfer to developing countries, may possibly be expected to remain in the industrialised countries to a greater extent than might otherwise have been the case.[22] In the long run, such possible

effects might, however, not always be in the interest of the parties
concerned and may delay the achievement of the New International
Economic Order. Obviously, the arguments advanced are of a speculative nature and further studies and more experience are needed to
substantiate these and other expectations concerning the potential
impact of technological innovations (and their application by MNEs)
on the international restructuring of industry.[23]

East-West enterprise-to-enterprise co-operation

Another aspect connected with the restructuring of industry is
the question of East-West enterprise-to-enterprise co-operation,
including joint ventures[24] and other linkages and their effects on
employment involving MNEs. Not much detailed knowledge exists on
this subject in the general literature on East-West industrial co-
operation.[25] An earlier ILO-commissioned study[26] suggested that
East-West enterprise-to-enterprise co-operation involving MNEs,
joint ventures, and other forms of MNE association with enterprises
in Eastern European countries would have positive employment effects
on both sides, and more so for the Western countries involved, in
the short and medium term, especially in slack periods when the
utilisation of existing capacities would be stimulated by this
co-operation. This suggests that in the economic situation
prevailing for the past few years such co-operation agreements
would act as a stimulus to employment in most Western industrialised
countries through a multiplier effect.

On the other hand, the report tends to suggest that in periods
of full or over-employment, the impact of East-West enterprise-to-
enterprise co-operation could have negative employment consequences
in the Western countries if the relevant production facilities
located in the Eastern European countries would out-produce
corresponding export production lines located in Western countries.

Reference may be made also to the subsidiaries of enterprises
of Eastern European origin in industrialised market economy
countries. While their number has grown in recent years, they are
not, for the time being at least, a major factor in the general
employment situation of the industrialised market economy
countries.[27]

Therefore, generally speaking, the existing literature puts
much more emphasis on East-West trade than on enterprise-to-
enterprise relationships. It should be noted that the arguments
put forward in the trade context are similar, i.e. that East-West
trade relations can have certain positive effects for both sides
especially in periods of under-utilisation of productive capacity.
However, according to some studies, a certain number of the
existing jobs in the West could be affected if, in time, Eastern
European products become more competitive and technologically
developed than in the past.[28]

It must be realised in discussing this subject that East-West
enterprise co-operation is not a field of discretionary activity
for multinational enterprises: "East-West co-operation agreements
lift normal activities between Western and Eastern enterprises to
the level of governmental concern. This is mainly a reflection of
the organisation of economic activities in centrally-planned
economies. Intergovernmental agreements of this sort are an attempt
to stabilise the external influence on the domestic long-term

economic planning; also, they are conscious attempts to obtain long-term assurances against disruptive and discriminative actions."[29] This certainly also applies, to a large extent, to the employment effects resulting from East-West enterprise-to-enterprise co-operation.

Information on the issue of "job export" and "employment export" by MNEs in country and case studies

The component studies contributed to the present research, and other case studies found in the available literature, can provide some further insight into this area of particular interest to industrialised countries.

The Belgian component study[30] noted that the investments abroad by Belgian multinationals are quite often the final step in a whole process of internationalisation which started with exports. Most initiatives for investments abroad apparently stem from an effort to defend the share of the market already secured by exports and to protected competitive positions against local and foreign enterprises. An investigation of 33 Belgian manufacturing MNEs (one-third of all Belgian MNEs) has shown that, in 38 per cent of the cases, the motives for going abroad were linked to these market considerations, as far as establishments in industrialised countries are concerned, and in 32 per cent of the cases, for the establishments implanted in developing countries. Among other motives advanced, 21 per cent in the context of subsidiary implantation in industrialised countries, and 26 per cent in the context of developing countries, were related to production costs. In general, cost factors were relatively more important for the implantation of subsidiaries in Asia, Africa and the Middle East while market considerations carried more weight in Latin America.

In assessing the domestic employment effects of Belgian MNE investments abroad, the methodology adopted by R. Hawkins for the United States[31] was applied with appropriate adaptation. This consisted of isolating partial effects according to a number of assumptions on the possibilities of alternative behaviour of the enterprises. The first factor that was considered in the Belgian study is the job displacement effect of foreign activities of Belgian MNEs.

On the assumption that the production of Belgian MNEs abroad could have been entirely replaced by exports, as of 1976 an estimated aggregate employment loss of 136,000 jobs is obtained. If one substracts from this total the employment created by Belgian mining MNEs abroad for which no substitution possibility through exports exists, the job displacement effect (still assuming a 100 per cent export substitution possibility for the remaining production) would drop to 125,863.

The hypothesis of an entire substitution of foreign production by exports is, however, completely unrealistic in the view of the authors of the Belgian study, since most of the investment abroad by Belgian MNEs was of a defensive nature. Therefore, the market position of the Belgian MNEs would be difficult to maintain by exports alone, especially where tariff and non-tariff barriers play an important role in the competitive situation. In addition, most of the foreign subsidiaries of Belgian industrial MNEs are situated in the neighbouring countries which have a product-mix which is very similar to the product-mix for the Belgian market. Therefore,

the authors adapted the range of the substitution coefficients to
the more realistic span of 10 to 30 per cent. If one then assumes
that 10 per cent of the Belgian production abroad could have been
exported from Belgium, that production in mining could not be sub-
stituted and that the imports from the foreign subsidiaries of
Belgian MNEs (estimated at 1,500 million Belgian francs or 2.5 per
cent of the total Belgian imports) could have been produced
locally, then the job displacement effect would have been 12,700
(until 1976). If one assumes another realistic substitution rate
of 30 per cent (instead of 100 per cent) then a further 39,000 jobs
could have been created in Belgium - had there been no establishment
of Belgian MNEs abroad.

The next effect examined in the Belgian study is the export
stimulation effect of foreign investment. This effect involves all
related employment in Belgium resulting from the existence of
production units abroad through their function as export platforms
for goods produced in Belgium. The export of capital goods necessary for the construction and expansion of subsidiaries abroad is
not considered here as it is assumed that orders for such capital
equipment would also have been placed if the additional productive
capacity had been installed in Belgium itself. More relevant here
is the export of semi-finished and finished goods to the subsidiaries abroad which might not otherwise have occurred. The
total exports by Belgian multinationals to their foreign subsidiaries were estimated at 31,000 million Belgian francs for 1976.
About one-quarter of such exports was composed of semi-manufactured
goods and three-quarters of fully manufactured goods. If one
assumes now that, in the best eventuality, at least 20 per cent of
the sales, and in the worst, 40 per cent of the sales to the
markets served by foreign subsidiaries of Belgian MNEs could not
have been produced in Belgium, one arrives at a positive employment
effect due to the export stimulation by foreign subsidiaries of
Belgian firms of between 2,650 and 5,300 employees.

The third effect considered is the home office employment
effect of the foreign investments. As supervisory and supporting
management activities remain concentrated in the parent company,
a number of additional people will be needed in the home country
to service the expanding subsidiaries abroad. The number of
managers at headquarters concerned with the affairs of the subsidiaries naturally varies with the degree of centralisation of
management and the degree of multi-nationality of each particular
company. Thus, the average number of managers with a management
responsibility for a foreign subsidiary was only 7 for the 30
responding Belgian MNEs. This average number multiplied by the
number of subsidiaries abroad yields a total home employment effect
estimate of 700 additional managerial jobs in Belgium, required as
a result of the implantation of MNE subsidiaries abroad.

Finally, there is the supporting firm employment effect, which
presented the greatest problems of evaluation. This effect relates
to the employment in firms and institutions which carry out supporting services for the foreign activities of Belgian MNEs. Government
institutions, such as the Belgian Corporation for International
Investment and the "Office National du Ducroire" (export and foreign
investment risk insurance) offer such (limited) employment opportunities. The same is true for private consulting firms and engineering
bureaux which offer a number of services to Belgian foreign
investors although they are not too numerous. It was not possible
in the Belgian case study to make a quantitative estimate of the

supporting firm employment effect for lack of suitable data. The same has to be said about the <u>indirect effect of the presence abroad of Belgian MNEs on the export of other Belgian enterprises</u>. Therefore, both the effects just referred to were not considered in the total evaluation by the authors of the Belgian component study.

The <u>total domestic employment effect</u> of the foreign investments of Belgian enterprises, calculated as a combination of the negative job displacement effect with the positive export stimulation and the home office employment effect, adds up to a total negative effect on the employment level in Belgium, of between 9,350 to 33,000 jobs (if one excludes the unrealistic assumption of a 100 per cent substitution). The first estimate (9,350) corresponds to an assumed substitution effect (i.e. the production which could possibly have been undertaken from the Belgian home base instead of being actually furnished by the foreign subsidiaries of Belgian MNEs) of 10 per cent; and the further assumption that 20 per cent of the exports were stimulated by the subsidiaries abroad. As regards the second figure (35,000), the substitution was estimated at 30 per cent, while the export stimulation via foreign subsidiaries was presumed to reach 40 per cent. If the two underlying hypotheses are not too unrealistic, then one may expect that the actual employment effect due to the two factors examined would probably lie somewhere between the two estimates indicated.

The authors of the Belgian study realise that, in making these estimates, some important factors are taken in isolation from the network of complex total economic relationships. Thus no account has been taken of the employment supporting effects of the foreign subsidiaries of Belgian MNEs for other firms, the indirect export stimulation effect for other firms relating from the increased Belgian industrial presence, and the supposedly beneficial dynamic effects of entrepreneurship, profitability and job security in those enterprises which are able to withstand international competitors in foreign markets. It has also to be borne in mind that the positive employment effects of foreign direct investment in Belgium have certainly, in general, been more important than any employment loss attributable to the investment of Belgian MNEs abroad.

Taking all these elements together, it is the authors' view that one can undoubtedly assume that, in the total analysis, the phenomenon of multinational enterprises has had a positive effect on the employment level in Belgium during the last decade or so.

In the same perspective of a total analysis of the MNE phenomenon, it has also been stressed in the Belgian study that a certain balance between outward and inward investment of MNEs seems important for the maintenance of a suitable volume of employment in the country. The authors of the study express some fear that outgoing investments by Belgian MNEs could in the longer-run have a negative impact on domestic employment should the present tendency of small amounts of incoming foreign investments continue for some time (assuming that other elements in the economic environment remain unchanged).[32] Obviously, the particular ratio and composition of domestic and foreign MNEs in Belgium means that such arguments cannot be generalised and applied everywhere.

The component study for the Federal Republic of Germany[33] notes that in a sample of German multinational enterprises surveyed by Fröbel[34], the number of workers employed in the foreign subsidiaries of these enterprises increased five-fold between 1961 and 1975 while their employees in the Federal Republic rose by approximately one-quarter (if only German workers are considered) and nearly by one-half if "guest-workers" (foreign workers) are also included. The study by Fröbel et al indicates, however, that for the period 1966-1976, German investments abroad continued to be made for the purpose of expansion (widening investment), while investment in the Federal Republic of Germany itself was largely for replacement and rationalisation, with a reduction of employment (deepening investment) in the case of many individual multinationals.[35]

Looking more specifically into the question of a possible substitution of foreign MNE production by corresponding investment in the Federal Republic of Germany, another study reviewed in the component study[36] indicates that precise estimates on this matter do not exist. It argues, however, that in some cases, it is rather obvious that the decision by an enterprise to invest and produce in a foreign country rather than to export to it, cannot have had substantial negative domestic employment repercussions. It is pointed out in this context, for instance, that half of the German-owned subsidiaries in the chemical industry in other industrialised countries, and the majority of subsidiaries in the electronics and metal sectors in EEC countries, are the result of take-overs by German MNEs of existing enterprises. Workers already employed in these firms, it is said, can hardly be considered to be taking jobs away from workers in the Federal Republic of Germany. A similar situation is noted with regard to MNE investments abroad designed to surmount trade barriers. In such cases, a product "made in Germany" is hardly a viable alternative to one produced by a foreign subsidiary of a German MNE, i.e. here too no jobs are exported. According to the study, even certain "offensive investments", which are not made with the prime consideration of protecting markets, may assume increasingly a defensive character over a period of time (therefore substituting fewer potential exports and hence fewer hypothetically exported jobs).

With regard to foreign MNEs in the Federal Republic of Germany, the study notes that the major question is obviously what the individual sectors involved would look like had these MNEs not appeared. Would domestic firms have replaced them in employment terms? In the view of the study cited, this seems unlikely to have happened in certain sectors such as the petroleum industry. Similarly, in the food and beverage industry where a few foreign firms hold 50 per cent of the capital, such an assumption is regarded by the authors as unlikely. In the chemical industry the position is, however, rather different. It is noted that, in this industry, in the absence of foreign MNEs, powerful German multinationals would probably have been capable, sooner or later, of stepping into the market. In the computer industry, on the other hand, it was felt that no domestic firm would have been in a position to replace an enterprise such as IBM in the past couple of years; and thus without IMB in the Federal Republic of Germany, the corresponding high technology products would have had to be imported (with a proportional loss of employment). These considerations, while to some degree speculative, are in the view of the author of the component study, the closest that researchers have come in attempting to verify the "non-MNE hypothesis" in the Federal Republic.

Basing itself on statistics contained in the documentation reviewed, the study concludes that, between 1961 and 1975, while German-owned multinational enterprises in general, expanded more in low-wage countries than in their home country, both from the point of view of production and employment, increases also took place in the over-all employment level of MNEs in Germany (or at least this level has been maintained). Such evidence contradicts, in the author's view, the thesis of large-scale permanent "employment exports"; but it does not exclude transfers of particular production lines, which certainly have occurred in the period in question.

The component study for the United Kingdom notes the absence of specific data which would make it possible to verify whether or not capital exports of UK-based MNEs have had negative domestic job effects. Some pointers in this matter can, however, be obtained from the record of major UK companies having substantial overseas interests.

At the end of 1977, 118 out of the 250 largest industrial firms in the United Kingdom, as listed in The Times 1000[37], were UK-owned and had at least three overseas manufacturing facilities. These firms may be considered as the major group of UK-based multinationals. Their employment record over the period 1971-75 was accordingly examined in the component study, with a view to comparing these figures with the available official statistics.

At the end of 1975 the 118 enterprises in question employed 2,527,000 people in the United Kingdom, and a further (estimated) one million overseas.[38] They had practically all expanded abroad during the first half of the 1970s and had added approximately 150,000 employees to their payroll in foreign countries in the four years 1971-75. At the same time, they had added about 80,000 employees to their payroll in the United Kingdom. Thus, employment-wise, they were clearly growing much faster abroad than at home, both in absolute and relative terms.

In the view of the author of the UK study[39], a large proportion of the jobs, at least in the UK, were added through acquisitions, although he found it difficult to determine the precise employment impact of these acquisitions. Nevertheless, the over-all impression of the author is that acquisitions are not the dominant factor for the employment performance of MNEs in the United Kingdom. Naturally, unadjusted employment figures are of relatively little use in determining whether or not jobs were actually being exported from the United Kingdom by the firms in question; yet the fact that the MNEs included in the sample, taken as a whole, added to the United Kingdom employment base during a period of over-all decline, suggests, in the author's opinion, that they are not the 'run-away' employers they are sometimes alleged to be.

Aggregates obviously tend to obscure wide differences in behaviour among the industrial sectors. Therefore, after a classification of the enterprises by industry, employment in the 118 United Kingdom MNEs was compared to employment in foreign-controlled firms and in the remainder of British industry. Although, for all the reasons mentioned above, these data can be considered as no more than initial approximations, both as regards the acquisitive behaviour of the large MNEs and their ability to maintain or increase employment, it can be seen that (except in the metal trades), the foreign firms systematically increased employment in the United Kingdom from 1971 to 1975. For the UK-based MNEs, employment has risen in five out of the thirteen industries analysed. In industries where such MNE employment has declined, it has generally fallen at a slower pace than in the rest of British industry. The only major exception is the automobile industry.

It is noted that in one or two sectors, notably food, drink and tobacco, the changes recorded have more to do with acquisitions than with real expansion. Rough estimates of the number of employees affected by these acquisitions suggest, even when adjusted, that the MNEs grew while the other enterprises declined. In a few other sectors, chemicals for example, the figures are critically influenced by the behaviour of a single major employer.

Over-all, in all sectors, the dominant impression of the author is that employment has benefited from close foreign ties (whether those of British or foreign-based multinationals) and has suffered from a lack of them. This conclusion is, in the author's view, not surprising since MNEs without successful products do not venture abroad. The author considers that, in the United Kingdom context, the incoming firms are among the world's best and those venturing abroad are among the country's best and most resilient (although there exist exceptions to this statement).

Even allowing for the possibility of distortion due to growth by acquisition of United Kingdom firms, the author holds that the record indicates that the over-all economic and employment effect in the United Kingdom of the presence of foreign MNEs has been beneficial and the same applies, in his judgment, to the UK-based MNEs.

The Swedish component study[40] is concerned with a micro-analysis of two Swedish multinational enterprises. It examines the likely effects on employment of realistic alternative invest-ment behaviour of these enterprises by asking the question: what would have happened, in employment terms, in the domestic produc-tion units of the enterprises had they opted for a partial replace-ment of their foreign production by exports from Sweden? Somewhat simplified, the findings of the study can be concisely stated as follows: in the short run, domestic employment would have increased to some degree had part of the products been exported from Sweden; but in the longer run manufacturing subsidiaries abroad would be more effective and, therefore, preferable also from the viewpoint of the future employment security of the firms' domestic labour force.

The component study for the United States[41] reviews the considerable body of specific research on domestic job losses and gains through the foreign activities of US-based multinationals. The results of this review are summarised hereafter. An early study by W.G. Dewald used aggregated data covering the period 1958-1974 for the United States' economy as a whole. It found "a strong positive association between imports, employment and income and a lack of association between the unemployment rate and imports, contrary to the neo-mercantilist hypothesis that exports gain jobs and imports cost jobs."[42] As a variation on this theme, another author, S. Magee, implies a "non-issue" conclusion in his observa-tions that workers who lose jobs from MNEs are not unlike those losing jobs from non-MNEs and are thus not entitled to any special consideration. In addition, Magee considers that the numbers of jobs involved are not very important, globally speaking.[43]

One of the first of the more detailed "job counting" studies
on the domestic employment effects of US MNE expansion abroad was
published by the Industrial Union Department, AFL-CIO, and prepared
by Ruttenberg and associates in 1971.[44] Using data from the Bureau
of Labor Statistics, US Department of Labor, Ruttenberg balanced
jobs generated in the growth of merchandise exports against those
which would have been required to produce US imports which compete
with domestic products. From 1966 to 1969, the US Bureau of Labor
estimated that employment, related to exports, grew from 2.5 million
to 2.7 million while jobs which would have been required to replace
US production-competing imports rose from 1.8 million to 2.5 million.
The net effect of these two considerations represents a loss of
500,000 US jobs, according to the author.[45] Goldfinger updated the
Ruttenberg job loss estimates with the identification of another
400,000 lost job opportunities during 1970 and 1971, the 1966-1971
total then growing to 900,000 jobs. He linked these findings both
to the imbalanced growth in US exports and imports, and to the
nature and growth of the US MNEs.[46]

Responding to the Ruttenberg/Goldfinger studies, several
business-related groups also undertook special studies on the
employment effects of US MNEs.[47] Thus, the National Foreign Trade
Council, Inc., surveyed in 1970 its member MNEs and collected data
on reasons for investing abroad, the domestic manufacturing employment effects of such decisions, and the long-term effect on US jobs
of the expansion of export opportunities as a result of the presence
of US-owned manufacturing facilities overseas.[48] The study
concluded that foreign MNE investments did not occur because of
lower labour costs abroad but because of market considerations;
that US-owned, foreign-based facilities resulted in increased
exports of US-made goods (often "more sophisticated" products than
otherwise); and that US exports and US domestic employment rose as
did foreign direct investment.

Following these initial studies three major reports have sub-
sequently appeared on the topic: a study conducted by the US
Tariff Commission (1973), a study by R. Frank and R. Freeman
sponsored by the US Department of Labor, State and Treasury (1975)
and a New York University research project "Economic Effects of
Multinational Corporations", under the direction of R. Hawkins
(1976).

The US Tariff Commission study presented three different
estimates of the US employment effects of direct foreign investments[49] which relate to differing assumptions on price competitiveness and other product market conditions confronting US MNEs.
Depending on the assumptions retained, the net US job impact of the
MNEs varied considerably (from a loss of 1,297,000 to an increase
of 629,000[50] for the period under consideration (1970).

Frank and Freeman took issue with some methodological features
of the US Tariff Commission study. They developed estimates of
domestic-to-foreign production cost ratios and market power (i.e.,
competitiveness of firms in an industry) and used these to estimate
a "home-foreign substitution ratio" for 15 different industries
which identified the portion of foreign employment that would have
been achieved in the United States had there been no foreign investment. Combining these ratios with production estimates predicated
on 1966-1973 foreign investment levels by industry, yielded
estimates for jobs created had the investments been US domestic
investments and the jobs created in domestic supporting industries.

These, less the number of jobs lost as import-supporting activities were eliminated, yielded, in the calculation of Frank and Freeman, an approximation of over one million domestic jobs lost that could be associated with United States' foreign direct investments abroad.[51]

The Hawkins' study utilised US Department of Commerce data collected in 1966 and 1970 on US multinationals and considered the relationships between the shares of alternative suppliers (i.e. exports from the US, sales by US-owned foreign subsidiaries, sales by non-US indigenous suppliers, and third-country imports) in 12 individual national markets.[52] It assumed constant market shares during 1966-1970 unless a competitive imbalance occurred among the suppliers, with the gain or loss of each supplier's sales vis-a-vis alternative sources calculated using 1966 weights. The US market was similarly analysed - with three suppliers identified: imports from US-owned subsidiaries in the same 12 national markets, imports from all other sources, and indigenous production.

The net gains or losses in US production for export, relative to the roles of foreign subsidiaries and resultant imports from such subsidiaries, vary considerably by industry according to Hawkins' calculations. As an over-all conclusion Hawkins observed that, according to his analysis, "... total US jobs have not suffered at the expense of US foreign affiliate operations. But some industries have lost output and jobs while others have gained to a greater degree ...".[53]

Although it is obvious that the results of the studies reviewed depend heavily on the assumptions chosen - and it would be difficult to obtain consensus on these - one can concur with the author of the US component study in that they have had at least the merit of identifying a number of issues to be considered in the context.[54] Additionally, they have also provided estimates for specific elements of importance to the question of employment change related to the activities of MNEs, whether these are generally accepted or not. Unfortunately, many of these estimates are somewhat dated by now; and it is, therefore, of interest that Kujawa in the US component study for the present project has attempted to assess the US employment effects of MNEs over the period 1973-1978, although he does not reopen the job export debate as such and limits his analysis to a comparison of the direct employment trends by category of enterprise and industry.[55] The results obtained by Kujawa suggest that, in this period, the US MNEs compare favourably with non-multinational enterprises as regards their domestic employment performance;[56] and that the shift within MNEs towards a greater component of professional and technical employment (i.e. on a higher average level of qualifications) continued, a result which is consistent with the findings in earlier studies.[57] Kujawa adds some estimates on the US employment effects of foreign MNEs, which have grown rapidly during the 1970s to reach a level of $40,800 million, i.e. approximately 24 per cent of US direct investment abroad. United States' subsidiaries of foreign enterprises employed over half a million people in 1974, 95 per cent of whom were US citizens. This figure has increased since. No exact recent survey data exists, however; and it is naturally impossible to arrive at a reliable estimate by simply linking this matter to the increase of direct foreign investment owing to (unknown) changes in the average capital/labour ratio.

As an over-all conclusion, from the more specific calculations reviewed, it can be noted, leaving extreme assumptions about alternatives to foreign investment/expansion of MNEs aside[58], that the effects of MNE expansion abroad on the total domestic employment volume in the industrialised home countries in question have probably not been very important, generally and proportionately, either in a positive or a negative sense. Rather than having a large affect on employment levels, foreign MNE expansion has certainly had a much greater impact on the structure of employment in the home country operations of MNEs during the last two decades or so, a subject dealt with in Chapter III of the present report.

Notes

[1] See OECD: The impact of the newly industrializing countries on production and trade in manufacturing (Paris, 1979), and Lawrence G. Franko: A survey of the impact of manufactured exports from industrializing countries in Asia and Latin America (Washington, National Planning Association, 1979).

[2] Dimitri Germidis (ed.): International subcontracting: A new form of investment (Paris, OECD Development Centre, 1980).

[3] See, for example, Robert Stobaugh, et al: Nine investments abroad and their impact at home: case studies in multinational enterprises and the US economy (Boston, Harvard Business School, 1976).

[4] See the findings of the "Systek series" in Raymond Vernon: Manager in the international economy (New Jersey, Englewood Cliffs, 1972). The "Systek series" refers to a number of case studies made possible through the co-operation of anonymous enterprises, designated as Systek International (A), (B), (C) and (D) in which names and figures have been disguised.

[5] A recent publication enlarges on this point as follows: "Without denying that the phenomenon exists, we [the authors] would argue that it is a mistake to put too much emphasis on it. What really matters is that the conditions underlying the world economy have changed. The multinationals are reacting to these changes, not creating them. Perhaps the classic example of this kind of enforced reaction was provided by the leading American television manufacturer, Zenith. This company led the way in aggressively trying to fight off Japanese imports in the early 1970s but in the face of superior Japanese competition (cheaper labour, superior design and production technology, and some alleged dumping), Zenith's US rivals were tempted offshore. Finally, in 1977, Zenith could hold out no longer and was forced into Taiwan and Mexico as well. This is a bleak demonstration of realities in today's global economy. Once an industry like television manufacture matures, companies in high-wage economies can only maintain jobs there by further innovation or by winning protectionist measures from their parent governments. Otherwise, they are faced with price competition from foreign companies - be they Japanese, European, or even from the NICs themselves - which increasingly cut their assembly costs by transferring key parts of their operations to low-wage economies." - in Louis Turner, Colin I. Bradford, Lawrence G. Franko, Neil McMullen and Stephen Woolcock: Living with the newly industrialised countries, Chatham House Papers, No. 7 (London, Royal Institute of International Affairs, 1980).

[6] Ibid.

[7] J.M. Finger: "Tariff provisions for off-shore assembly and the exports of developing countries", in Economic Journal (Cambridge), vol. 85 (June 1975), pp. 365-371.

[8] A list of MNEs which have engaged in off-shore operations has been compiled by the United Nations Conference on Trade and Development and is presented in UNCTAD: International subcontracting arrangements in electronics between developed market-economy countries and developing countries (New York, 1975; Sales No.: E.75.II.D.17), pp. 17-18.

[9] Deepak Nayyar: "Transnational corporations and manufactured exports from poor countries", Economic Journal (Cambridge), Vol. 88 (March 1978), pp. 64-72.

[10] United Nations: Transnational corporations in world development, op. cit., p. 237.

[11] OECD: The impact of the new industrializing countries on production and trade in manufacturers (Paris, 1979).

[12] Harvard Multinational Enterprise Project Data, in L. Franko: The European multinationals, op. cit., p. 221.

[13] Calculated from US Department of Commerce and World Bank data. See Lawrence G. Franko: "Financing economic development", in Journal of World Trade Law, March-April 1978, esp. pp. 128-129.

[14] Calculated from US Department of Commerce: Survey of current business (February 1977), estimates of exports of US MNE affiliates, and World Bank estimates of total manufactured exports from LDCs.

[15] Similar precise data as in the US case are not available for non-US MNEs' exports from LDCs, but a rough indication can be obtained for them from the Harvard subsidiary census in the early 1970s which showed Japanese-based MNEs to be somewhat more inclined, and European-based MNEs somewhat less inclined than US-based MNEs, to use their subsidiaries in developing countries as export bases. See also L.G. Franko: Multinational enterprise: the international division of labour and the developing countries, op. cit., and Y. Tsurumi: The Japanese are coming, op. cit.

[16] Jean Currie: Investment: The growing role of export processing zones (London, the Economist Intelligence Unit, June 1979), EIU Special Report No. 64, pp. 5 ff. See also Chapter V on Export Processing Zones in ILO: Employment effects of multinational enterprises in developing countries, op. cit.

[17] Ben Evers, Gerard de Groot, Willy Wagenmans: Hong Kong: Development and perspective of a clothing colony, Netherlands Development Research Institute, March 1977, translated summary, mimeo.

[18] Herbert Werner: "Probleme der internationalen Arbeitsteilung", in: Materialien aus der Arbeitsmarkt- und Berufsforschung (Erlangen), Heft 9/1979, pp. 3-7.

[19] Ibid., p. 7.

[20] Information on production transfers and connected job losses, "disinvestments" and the cancellation by MNEs of decisions to invest are found in particular in trade union and related sources. For recent references to these matters see Centrale des Metallurgistes FGTB: "Les sociétés multinationales", CMB INFORM, Nov.-Dec. 1980, pp. 39-40.

[21] Point mentioned in several memoranda received from governments in reply to the ILO survey referred to in footnote 7, Chapter I.

[22] Juan F. Rada: The impact of microelectronics: A tentative appraisal of information technology (Geneva, ILO, 1980).

[23] These problems are studied in detail by the Technology and Employment Branch of the ILO's Employment and Development Department, see the entries under "Technology and employment" in ILO: Bibliography of published research of the World Employment Programme (Geneva, third edition, 1980), pp. 14-27. Extensive studies on the effects of technological changes, their effects on world situations and the structural adjustments involved are being carried out in various industrialised countries (e.g. Australia, Austria, France, Fed. Rep. of Germany, Hungary, Japan, Sweden, Switzerland, the United Kingdom and the USSR). See in this connection "Structural adjustment in developed countries", in Industry and Development (New York, UNIDO, 1979), No. 3, pp.78-86.

[24] A recent analysis of joint ventures in Eastern European countries involving multinational enterprises is given in Leon Zurawicki: Multinational enterprises in the West and East (Alphen aan den Rijn (Netherlands), Sijthoff Noordhoff, 1979).

[25] See, for instance, East-West industrial co-operation (New York, United Nations, 1979; Sales No.E.79.II.E.25).

[26] F.H. Fleck and H. Bortis: Effects of East-West industrial co-operation on employment and on the general conditions of workers; paper, prepared in 1977, for the ILO (unpublished).

[27] These subsidiaries are found, for instance, in banking, manufacturing assembly, electronic and electrical industry. Different ownership patterns exist. Some of the banking subsidiaries are wholly-owned, but most subsidiaries seem to be established as joint ventures with varying ratios of capital ownership. An overview of recent developments is found in Carl H. McMillan: "The rise of the Eastern bloc multinationals" in International Management (December 1980), pp. 19-23.

[28] Dieter Masberg: Beschäftigungswirkungen der Ost-West-Wirtschaftsbeziehungen in der Bundesrepublik Deutschland und den Niederlanden (Nijmegen, 1979).

[29] United Nations Industrial Development Organisation: Industry 2000 - new perspectives: Collected background papers, Vol. 2, International Industrial Enterprise Co-operation (Vienna, 1979), p. 35.

[30] Van Den Bulcke and Halsberghe, op. cit., cf. pp. 39-49 in particular.

[31] R. Hawkins: Job displacement and the multinational firm: a methodological review (Washington, Center for Multinational Studies, 1972) and Multinational investment in manufacturing and domestic performance (Washington, Center for Multinational Studies, 1972).

[32] Belgian component study, op. cit.

[33] Bailey, op. cit., p. 14.

[34] Fröbel, et al: The new international division of labour, op. cit., Chapter 10, p. 185 ff.

[35] Fröbel, ibid., p. 288.

[36] Jungnickel, op. cit.

[37] The Times 1000 (1978-79) (London, Times Books Ltd., 1978). 1978).

[38] Exact data on overseas employment were available for 77 of the firms.

[39] Stopford, op. cit.

[40] G.L. Jordan and F. Vahlne, op. cit.

[41] Kujawa, op. cit.

[42] W.G. Dewald: "Do imports and exports affect the number of jobs?" in Bulletin of Business Research (The Ohio State University, Center for Business and Economic Research, June 1975), p. 6.

[43] Stephen P. Magee: "Jobs and the multinational corporation: The home-country perspective", in Robert G. Hawkins (ed.): The economic effects of multinational corporations, Volume 1 (Research in International Business and Finance), (Greenwich, Conn., JAI Press, 1979), p. 11.

[44] Stanley H. Ruttenberg and Associates: Needed: A constructive foreign trade policy (Washington, D.C., Industrial Union Department, AFL-CIO, 1971).

[45] Ibid., pp. 62-63.

[46] Nathaniel Goldfinger: "An American trade union view of international trade and investment", in Duane Kujawa (ed.): American labor and the multinational corporation (New York, Praeger, 1973), p. 35.

[47] For a more detailed review of several of these studies, see Michael Jay Jedel and John H. Stamm: "The battle over jobs: An appraisal of recent publications on the employment effects of U.S. multinational corporations", in Duane Kujawa (ed.): American labor and the multinational corporation, op. cit., pp. 144-191.

[48] National Foreign Trade Council: The impact of U.S. foreign direct investment on U.S. employment and trade: an assessment of critical claims and proposals (New York, 1971).

[49] "The impact of the MNCs on US labor: Job creation vs job destruction", in US Senate, Committee on Finance: Implications of multinational firms for world trade and investment and for US trade and labor (Washington, D.C., U.S. Government Printing Office, 1973), pp. 645-72.

[50] Including the employment effect attributed to foreign direct investments in the United States.

[51] Robert H. Frank and Richard T. Freeman: "The impact of United States direct foreign investment on domestic unemployment", a report on a research project sponsored by the U.S. Departments of Labor, State and Treasury (mimeographed), May 1975. The report was published as Distributional effects of multinational enterprises (New York, Basic Books, 1978).

[52] Robert G. Hawkins: Jobs, skills and US multinationals, a statement to the Subcommittee of International Economic Policy, Committee on International Relations, U.S. House of Representatives (mimeographed), February 1976, esp. pp. 10-15.

[53] Ibid., p. 17 and 19.

[54] Kujawa, US component study, op. cit., p. 15 (listed in the appendix).

[55] Ibid., pp. 22-28.

[56] In the same vein, according to a recent Business International study, the job export hypothesis was refuted since US enterprises investing abroad had not reduced employment at home. See Business International: The effects of US corporate foreign investment: The 'Fortune 100' 1960-75 (New York, 1977), pp. 1-2, as well as other publications in this series.

[57] This trend is also mentioned in some of the earlier ILO sectoral studies. See for instance ILO: Social and labour practices of some European-based multinationals in the metal trades, op. cit., p.115.

[58] One alternative, other than exports, viz. licensing, is referred to in a recent study as a "second-best strategy", see P.J. Buckley and H. Davis: The place of licensing in the theory and practice of foreign operations (University of Reading, Nov. 1979; Discussion Papers in International Investment and Business Studies No 47; mimeographed). For a review of studies relevant to the motives of MNE investments abroad, see J.P. Agarwal: "Determinants of foreign direct investment: A survey", in Weltwirtschaftliches Archiv (Kiel), Vol. 116, No. 4, 1980, pp. 739-773.

CHAPTER V

CONCLUSIONS

In practically all industrialised market economy countries,
most of which are both home and host countries of MNEs, multinational enterprises hold a significant share of employment,
especially in manufacturing but also in the service sector. Great
variations exist, however, in the relative importance of employment
provided by multinationals, in particular foreign multinationals, in
these countries. Thus, employment in subsidiaries of foreign enterprises (fully or partly foreign-owned) accounted in the mid-1970s
for a low of less than two per cent of total manufacturing employment in Japan against about 15 per cent in the Federal Republic of
Germany, more than 30 per cent in Belgium and around 40 per cent
in Canada. Not surprisingly, interest in foreign enterprises as
contributors to public employment policy goals as well as concern
over the employment impact of their investment policies are clearly
linked to their national and sectoral shares.

Employment figures relating to foreign MNEs do not take account
of the importance of employment provided by multinationals in their
home countries. As a matter of fact, in many of the industrialised
market economy countries, the employment share of domestic multinationals considerably exceeds that of the foreign multinationals
and is, therefore, a major determinant for the employment effects
of the total MNE phenomenon. Even if, for the estimate, a restricted
definition is applied with regard to the minimum number of foreign
production subsidiaries (and the percentage share capital which must
be held in such subsidiaries) and the size which an enterprise must
have in order to qualify as an MNE - manufacturing MNEs (domestic
and foreign combined) appear to account for over 40 per cent of
industrial employment in nine out of the twelve most industrialised
market economy countries.

Cautious estimates for the mid-1970s would place employment in
multinational enterprises in the manufacturing industry at some
25 to 30 million in the industrialised market economy countries
taken as a whole (depending on the criteria chosen for defining
such enterprises). It can be assumed that approximately another
10 million would have to be added to this figure if MNE employment
in service industries, such as banking, insurance, hotel and
retailing chains and advertising agencies were included.

Employment in multinational enterprises (and their share in
employment, sales, turnover, value added, investments, etc.)
increased markedly during the 1950s and even more so in the 1960s,
which were characterised by unprecedented general economic growth
in most of the countries under reference. The growth in employment
in MNEs has slowed in the late 1970s, although there are indications
that MNE shares in total activities have continued to increase.

The phenomenon of the multinational enterprise has changed in
the last decades in terms of distribution of national origin of
enterprises and, in part, sectors of operation and location.
Furthermore, new types of MNE relations, in the form of non-capital
linkages, enterprise-to-enterprise agreements, co-production agreements, management contracts etc., have also appeared. However,
these new patterns of MNE activity have mainly emerged under the

impact of the different economic and political environment in
developing countries and in certain East European countries. On
the other hand, in the industrialised market economy countries the
main linkage of MNE parent companies to affiliates abroad has
remained capital ownership, established through both new investments and acquisitions.

Examining the various industrialised countries, a differen-
tiated distribution pattern emerges with regard to the relative
importance of employment in foreign and domestic MNEs in the mid-
1970s. First, there is a group of countries in which employment in
foreign-owned subsidiaries is a large and significant factor in
total manufacturing employment in the host country. Countries such
as Austria, Belgium and Canada are typical examples. On the other
hand, there is a second group of countries where employment in the
MNEs with headquarters in these countries is much more substantial
than that in foreign enterprises. Predominant here is the situation
of the United States, with approximately 7 million employed in
domestic MNEs as against only 650,000 employees in foreign-owned
enterprises (at the beginning of the 1970s), followed by the
Federal Republic of Germany (1.5 million in German MNEs vs. 470,000
in the larger foreign-owned enterprises in 1974), the United Kingdom
(2.5 million vs 926,000 in 1975) and Sweden (316,000 vs 100,000 in
foreign-owned MNEs in 1976). An extreme situation is found in
Luxembourg where the bulk of manufacturing employment is accounted
for by one large Luxembourg-headquartered MNE. It is estimated
that a third or more of manufacturing employment in countries such
as the United States, Switzerland, the Netherlands, the United
Kingdom and Sweden is in the home-country operations of MNEs. Also,
in Canada, which is usually thought of as a MNE host country, nearly
30 per cent of the manufacturing employment is provided by Canadian
MNEs. (Almost three-quarters of Canadian industrial employment
appears to be in Canadian-owned and foreign-based MNEs combined.)
For Belgium, another major traditional host country of MNEs, it was
found that half as many people are employed in the domestic operations of Belgian MNEs as in foreign-owned enterprises.

Lastly, two other groupings of countries can be distinguished
if home country employment provided by domestic MNEs is compared
with employment provided by the same enterprises abroad (over-
lapping with the earlier groupings). In the mid-1970s, MNEs in a
number of countries employed as many as up to three times more
persons in their foreign operations as in operations in their home
country while the reverse observation could be made for another set
of countries. Examples of the first category are the Netherlands
(1 million employed abroad by the 37 largest Netherlands' MNEs and
362,000 at home), Switzerland (460,000 employees abroad in the 35
largest MNEs and 214,000 at home) and Belgium (182,000 employees
abroad in 96 MNEs and 163,000 at home). As regards Swedish MNEs,
their employment abroad and at home was almost at the same level.
If one considers the usually large scale of MNE operations, it is
understandable that MNEs based in the smaller countries have a great
tendency to venture abroad and also to become more "multinational"
with regard to their employment effects.

The opposite seems true for MNEs home-based in a group of
larger countries. Thus, by the mid-1970s, domestic MNEs in the
United States, the United Kingdom and the Federal Republic of
Germany were providing much more employment at home than were their
subsidiaries abroad (i.e. approximately 6.7 million vs. 3.3 million,
2.5 million vs 1 million, and 1.5 million vs 500,000, respectively).

In the case of Canada, 540,000 persons were employed by domestic MNEs at home as against some 360,000 in their foreign subsidiaries. Perhaps not surprisingly, it can thus be observed that the larger countries whose MNEs have relatively fewer employees abroad than at home are at the same time, those countries in which domestic MNEs provide the bulk of the total MNE employment.

The available data, including those from a special ILO survey undertaken among a sample of more than 250 major Australian, Canadian, European and Japanese MNEs, indicate that, in approximately the last 10-15 years, employment in foreign operations of MNEs has generally tended to grow more rapidly than in their home country operations, such increases being most marked in the developing host countries. Nevertheless, in terms of volume, both of investment and employment, the industrialised market economy countries remain the main area of MNE operations; they accounted, for instance, for three-quarters of the stock of all MNE investment in the mid-1970s. At the same time, where such information was available for the same period, it has been found that the employment trends of MNEs in their main industrialised home countries has, on the whole, been broadly in line with the general trend in manufacturing. At times MNE employment increases were even greater than the general increases in employment, such as in the United States, the Federal Republic of Germany, the United Kingdom, Switzerland and Sweden, to mention some examples; the foreign employment expansion of multinational enterprises was thus not accompanied, over the longer-term period of the last 10-15 years, by a decrease in the employment volume in the home country operations. Therefore, the hypothesis of a large-scale "employment export" by these enterprises - understood here in the (limited) sense of a corresponding fall in the volume of domestic employment associated with the expansion of the volume of employment in MNE operations abroad - is not confirmed by the findings of this study, for the period and countries considered. Of course, the question of what would have happened to employment in the same industrialised home countries had MNEs not expanded, or expanded less, abroad is not answered by these comparisons.

Some particular case studies examined in the body of the report provide some indications on this question although they have given rise to controversy. These case examinations point both to the complexity of the "job export" and "employment export" issues if possible alternatives to foreign MNE expansion (such as exports) are considered and to the difficulties in establishing consensus about the underlying assumptions of the studies. In addition, there is the problem that the case examinations by their very nature isolate the area from the wider economic context, including government policies. In general, the case studies find a certain loss of manual jobs in the home country operations of MNEs, and an increase in white-collar jobs there, as being associated with the MNE expansion abroad. However, leaving the extreme estimates aside, and disregarding the methodological problems, such changes do not seem, in most situations, to have had a very sizeable impact on the total employment volume in the countries in question according to the study results. Perhaps, rather than providing unquestionable numerical assessments, a particular contribution of the case studies might be that they shed light on the critical and varying aspects involved.

One such critical aspect highlighted in the studies is that changes in job structures in MNEs may lead to imbalances in the labour market and, as in the case of structural change from other factors, may impose adjustment and social costs for the segments of the MNE labour force concerned (redundancy, unemployment, retraining, etc.). This entails hardships, especially for under-privileged groups in the labour market, including the less qualified, most affected by all structural change, whatever the numbers involved may be.

The global trends also observed do not contradict evidence of specific instances of transfers by MNEs of production lines and jobs both to other industrialised and to developing countries. Certainly, multinational enterprises contribute through their international investment policy (whether a result of discretionary decision or, apparently more often, under the pressure of market and cost developments), to the international restructuring of industry and employment. Still, MNEs are only one, although a particularly visible, agent for such change; and, according to the evidence on hand, they are, as such, a less important change agent than are international trade and subcontracting with which MNEs are, however, interrelated.

While most MNE growth took place in the 1950s and especially the 1960s, the relative importance of the MNEs in employment terms usually continued to increase in the 1970s. Thus, the proportion of the total manufacturing workforce employed in foreign MNE sub-sidiaries (the most readily available indicator) increase during the early 1970s - notably in Belgium (from 18 to 33 per cent) - but also, even if to a lesser degree, in the United Kingdom (from 10.3 to 12.4 per cent), in Sweden (from 4.1 to 5.7 per cent), in France (from 18 to 19 per cent) and in Finland (from 2.8 to 3.2 per cent). One of the factors associated with this trends appears to be the sector of MNE operation. Within manufacturing, MNEs seem to concentrate largely in growth industries, which are less affected than other industries by general economic slowdown and structural change. On the other hand, MNE presence is apparently relatively low in a variety of manufacturing industries which are presently facing considerable structural problems, including clothing and steel, or shipbuilding, in which non-multinational enterprises rather than MNEs, predominate. This is not to say, of course, that MNE activity does not exist at all in the industries which are going through a major employment decline in the industrialised world; but the data do suggest that the bulk of MNE activity has tended to be concentrated in sectors of relative (if, during the late 1970s especially, modest) employment growth or at least stability. Naturally, MNE association with these growth - or relative growth - sectors does not imply by itself any causal relationships.

More detailed statistics show, however, that at least in some cases, concentration in growth industries does not always completely explain the employment trends in MNEs. Certain variations in the performance of companies observable in the same industry seem to suggest that MNE performance may also in part be attributed to their organisational characteristics and strategies. Thus, in the United Kingdom, foreign enterprises seem to have increased employment in some industries from 1971 to 1975, while employment in both domestic MNEs and in non-MNEs in these industries tended to stagnate. On the other hand, in the Federal Republic of Germany, domestic MNEs increased their employment between 1966 and 1973 in the chemical industry while employment in foreign MNEs and in local firms declined.

It must be added also that some of the recent employment growth in MNEs in certain countries seems to be attributable to a greater extend than in the 1950s and 1960s to acquisitions rather than to new investment.

MNEs have been found to constitute a particular high proportion of activity and employment in industries making relatively intensive use of both technology and capital. Thus, MNEs loom large in industries such as chemicals, pharmaceuticals, petroleum refining, electrical and non-electrical machinery and transport equipment, especially automobiles and parts. The food, drink and tobacco industries also represent an important sector of MNE activity, especially for enterprises based in the United States and the United Kingdom. Incidentally, rather similar concentration patterns for MNEs are also found in the developing countries although primary production remains an important area of MNE activity there. The fact that multinationals are concentrated in growth sectors may not, of course, just be due to chance. Some of this concentration no doubt reflects deliberate choice and adaptation.

A tendency on the part of MNEs to be more sensitive than national firms to changing economic conditions, including world market influences, has been noted in several reports and component studies - with the possible corollary that they may also tend to react more quickly, in times of economic slowdown, with respect to manpower adjustments. However, employment security in MNEs does not seem to differ materially from that found in exclusively nationally operating firms, a fact probably explained, for the most part, by their rather wide integration into the local labour law and industrial relations setting.

As MNEs are increasingly to be found in capital-intensive industries and take a certain lead in research and development, their future growth potential for employment in the production sector of industrialised countries will be necessarily affected by this fact (although account must also be taken of their economic growth potential and their indirect employment effects). In fact, in virtually every industrialised host country for which the necessary indicators are available, the weight of foreign-owned enterprises in terms of manufacturing sales, value-added, wages and salaries paid, and total investment or gross capital formation, was greater than it was in employment (although in the more detailed analysis this seems largely associated with the sectors of operation). These considerations may be less important for multinational enterprises in the service sector (banking, insurance, etc.) and trade.

In the longer-term perspective, MNEs are found to both follow and influence in varying degrees the global sectoral dynamics of the economy in line with the economic restructuring of the primary, secondary and tertiary sectors, usually conceptualised as the maturing of industrial societies and their passage to a post-industrial stage - just as they have been found to be intimately linked with long-term change in international economic relations. The long-term restructuring process has become interwoven, in recent years, with the effects of recession on industrial employment; and in this respect too, MNEs, despite some specific trends, have been affected roughly in the same way as other enterprises.

Statistically, the question concerning exactly what part of structural change is due to broader factors and what to multi-nationals is perhaps unanswerable. Nonetheless, it is clear that, particularly in times of slow growth, any employment effects, including the employment effects resulting from MNE decisions, merit particular attention. As in the case of other enterprises, the need for MNEs to keep their manpower plans, as far as practicable, in harmony with national policies, to provide reasonable notice of changes in operations affecting employment, and to consult as appropriate with government authorities, employers' and workers' organisations and other workers' representatives, will remain principles of great social importance in the years to come. It is also clear that where well-developed, active labour policies exist in the enterprises and at large, based on an anticipatory rather than reactive approach, especially as regards manpower development and retraining, they can considerably help social adjustment to change, whatever its origin. Finally, as MNEs are a world-wide phenomenon, the analysis of the employment effects of MNEs in the industrialised market economy countries - the focus of this present report - needs to be supplemented by an analysis of their employment effects in developing countries. This is the subject of the forthcoming companion report to the present volume.

APPENDIX

COMPONENT STUDIES FOR RESEARCH PROJECT ON
EMPLOYMENT EFFECTS OF MULTINATIONAL ENTERPRISES

MULTI Working Papers*

Employment effects of multinational enterprises: A Belgian
case study (Working Paper No. 1)
by D. Van Den Bulcke and E. Halsberghe
ISBN 92-2-102265-X

Employment effects of multinational enterprises: A survey
of relevant studies relating to the Federal Republic of Germany
(Working Paper No. 2)
by P.J. Bailey
ISBN 92-2-102266-8

The indirect employment effects of multinational enterprises
in developing countries (Working Paper No. 3)
by Sanjaya Lall
ISBN 92-2-102280-3

Les effets des entreprises multinationales agro-alimentaires
sur l'emploi en Amérique latine (Working Paper No. 4)
by G. Arroyo, S. Gomes de Almeida and J.M. von Der Weid
ISBN 92-2-202268-8

Employment effects of multinational enterprises in the
United Kingdom (Working Paper No. 5)
by J.M. Stopford
ISBN 92-2-102269-2

Employment effects of foreign direct investments in ASEAN
countries (Working Paper No. 6)
by Y. Kuwahara, T. Harada and Y. Mizuno
ISBN 92-2-102270-6

Employment effects of multinational enterprises in Brazil
(Working Paper No. 7)
by M.L. Possas
ISBN 92-2-102271-4

Employment effects of multinational enterprises: A case
study of Kenya (Working Paper No. 8)
by R. Kaplinsky
ISBN 92-2-102272-2

The effects of multinational enterprises on employment in
India (Working Paper No. 9)
by U. Dar
ISBN 92-2-102277-3

Employment effects of multinational enterprises in Nigeria
(Working Paper No. 10)
by O. Iyanda and J.A. Bello
ISBN 92-2-102274-9

Employment effects of multinational enterprises in the
Philippines (Working Paper No. 11)
by C. Tanchoco-Subido
ISBN 92-2-102278-1

Employment effects of multinational enterprises: The case
of the United States (Working Paper No. 12)
by D. Kujawa
ISBN 92-2-102276-5

Domestic employment effects of direct investment abroad
by two Swedish multinationals (Working Paper No. 13)
by G.L. Jordan and J.-E. Vahlne
ISBN 92-2-102267-6

Multinational enterprises and employment-oriented
"appropriate" technologies in developing countries
(Working Paper No. 14)
by S. Watanabe
ISBN 92-2-102573-X

Multinational enterprises and employment in the Caribbean
(with special reference to Trinidad and Tobago)
(unpublished draft paper)
by T. Turner

Effets sur l'emploi des entreprises multinationales:
le cas de la Mauritanie (unpublished draft paper)
by P. Bonte

Les multinationales et l'emploi: le cas du Zaïre
(unpublished draft paper)
by D. Vandersteen and J.-C. Williame

---

 * Working papers contributed to the ILO's Multinational
enterprises programme (MULTI).

    Responsibility for the opinions expressed in working
papers rests with their authors.